Awaiting the Impossible

Awaiting the Impossible

*A Dialogue with Derrida, Deconstruction,
and the Endless Wait for Messiah*

SEE SENG TAN

Foreword by Gordon Wong

WIPF & STOCK · Eugene, Oregon

AWAITING THE IMPOSSIBLE
A Dialogue with Derrida, Deconstruction, and the Endless Wait for Messiah

Copyright © 2022 See Seng Tan. All rights reserved. Except for brief quotations in critical publications or reviews, no part of this book may be reproduced in any manner without prior written permission from the publisher. Write: Permissions, Wipf and Stock Publishers, 199 W. 8th Ave., Suite 3, Eugene, OR 97401.

Wipf & Stock
An Imprint of Wipf and Stock Publishers
199 W. 8th Ave., Suite 3
Eugene, OR 97401

www.wipfandstock.com

PAPERBACK ISBN: 978-1-6667-4162-9
HARDCOVER ISBN: 978-1-6667-4163-6
EBOOK ISBN: 978-1-6667-4164-3

APRIL 28, 2022 10:14 AM

This book is dedicated to my wonderful colleagues in International Students Inc. (ISI), who model what it means to walk daily with Christ and to serve him in his spirit and in truth.

Contents

Foreword by Gordon Wong | ix

Introduction | 1

1 Self Before Other | 7

2 Deconstruction's Promises (and Perils) | 25

3 Awaiting Deconstruction's Impossible God | 52

4 Hello from the Other Side | 86

Conclusion | 120

Bibliography | 129

Foreword

JACQUES DERRIDA, IN HIS book *Margins of Philosophy* (as translated by Alan Bass), writes in his opening chapter ("Différance"): "There is no simple answer to such a question." What Derrida wrote about the specific question concerning *Différance* might well be applied to the more general question that most of us would ask: What does "Deconstruction" mean? There is no simple answer to such a question. See Seng Tan in his book helps provide us with at least a partial answer to that question, and he is to be commended for trying to make that answer as simple as he can (but where *simple* is not to be misunderstood as *simplistic*). A 1st century writer advised his readers to "test everything; hold fast what is good. Abstain from every form of evil" (Paul of Tarsus, 1 Thessalonians 5:21-22 *English Standard Version*). Professor Tan has followed this sage advice, helping us consider what is good in Derrida's work of Deconstruction, while also urging us to abstain from what is not so good. It is a pleasure for me to commend this example of respectful and constructive dialogue which Professor Tan has given us.

THE REV. DR. GORDON WONG
Bishop, Methodist Church of Singapore

Introduction

If Jackie Met Jesus

The philosopher is someone whose desire and ambition are absolutely mad; the desire for power of the greatest politicians is absolutely minuscule and juvenile compared to the desire of the philosopher who, in a philosophical work, manifests both a design on mastery and a denunciation of mastery on a scale and to a degree that I find infinitely more powerful than can be found elsewhere . . . There is an adventure of power and unpower, a play of potence and impotence, a *size* of desire that seems to me, with the philosophers, much more impressive than elsewhere. It is out of proportion with other types of discourse, and sometimes even with all the rules of art.[1]

THIS BOOK IS AN attempt at a Christian engagement with the philosophy of deconstruction introduced by the late French intellectual Jacques Derrida, once described by *The New York Times*, no doubt overgenerously, as "perhaps the world's most famous philosopher—if not the only famous philosopher."[2] Born on July 15, 1930, in El Biar in French-ruled Algeria to a Jewish family, Jackie Derrida (he changed his name to Jacques at the start of his academic career) died on October 8, 2004, in Paris of pancreatic cancer. From the inception of Derrida's prodigious scholarship in the late 1960s, deconstruction has exerted an outsized influence over practically everything from arts and architecture, literature, music and entertainment, economics, society, politics, to even religion. Taken by many to denote

---

1. Derrida, *Points*, 139–40, italics original.
2. Smith, "Philosopher Gamely In Defense Of His Ideas."

the indiscriminate, irresponsible, and irreverent destruction of long-held philosophical, religious, and moral traditions by a postmodern generation, deconstruction has elicited alarmist and reactionary responses, not without reason, from evangelical Christians. That said, such responses tend either to caricaturize deconstruction negatively or ignore it altogether, fostering the unfortunate impression that postmodern sensibilities are best kept out of God's church and that any residue found within ought to be immediately exorcised. Consider this recent example: Writing for *Christianity Today* on the challenges facing evangelicalism today and the need for change, a church leader commented, "There have always been reformers in the church, and we did not call them deconstructors."[3] Noting that "the church needs reformation, not deconstruction," the author, without quite explaining what deconstruction is, summarily concluded that it harms rather than helps the church[4]—a perspective held by many evangelicals. Or consider this assessment from the conservative critic Roger Kimball: "Derrida's influence has been disastrous. He has helped foster a sort of anemic nihilism, which has given imprimaturs to squads of imitators who no longer feel that what they are engaged in is a search for truth, who would find that notion risible."[5] The implication from both those examples, and many others like them, is clear: *deconstruction destroys, period*.

That might well be the case, but my following inquiry suggests things are a lot more complicated than that. For one thing, in roundly dismissing deconstruction as a purely destructive force, the perspective rejects all possibility that any good can derive from deconstruction.[6] Nor does it offer any guidance to Christians on how they may engage intellectually and missionally with postmodern audiences, many of whom can be found in our congregations—or at least the ones who have not yet left the church, disillusioned with the Christian faith.[7] There is reason to believe that postmodern apathy and indifference toward Christianity rests in no small measure on the failure of evangelicals to really understand postmodern

---

3. Warren, "Church Needs Reformation, Not Deconstruction."

4. Warren, "Church Needs Reformation, Not Deconstruction."

5. Cited in Stephens, "Jacques Derrida."

6. For instance, the philosopher of religion Carl Raschke has suggested that the postmodernist revolution in philosophy "has tendered an environment where the Christian gospel can at last be disentangled from the centuries-long gnarl of scientism, rationalism, secularism, humanism, and skepticism." Raschke, *Next Reformation*, 21.

7. Seidal, "Love Letter to #Exvangelicals and Those Deconstructing Their Toxic Faith."

concerns, that is, understanding that stems from a careful consideration of deconstruction's most significant claims rather than simplistic reliance on the echo chamber of cliched and often unreliable secondhand opinions. For another thing, the perspective ignores a rather surprising key fact: the primary motivation behind Derrida's relentless deconstructive labors had all along been *religious* in nature.[8] In his widely cited 1993 essay entitled "Circumfession," Derrida famously lamented, even as his reputation as a global academic superstar continued to skyrocket, that his work has been "read less and less well over almost twenty years, *like my religion about which nobody understands anything.*"[9] Thus understood, deconstruction is effectively demythologization because of Derrida's preoccupation, call it his magnificent obsession, with the holy and the messianic. Quite the unexpected revelation indeed from a man whose atheistic credentials stemmed from his long-held skepticism and suspicion with orthodox religions or what he termed "concrete messianisms." It turns out that deconstruction, at least in Derrida's hands, was waiting for Messiah. It still is, as practiced today by influential deconstructionists like the American continental philosopher John D. Caputo, who continue to carry the torch of Derridean deconstruction.

And if so, what expressions of affirmative faith might deconstruction welcome, given, as has been argued, that it "opens up the space for an affirmative faith to occur and be professed"?[10] Is deconstruction's unconditional hospitality to the other sufficient grounds on which it and Christianity might conceivably build common cause? Crucially, does deconstruction's quest for the messianic pave a way, does it build a bridge, toward the profession of an affirmative faith *in Christ*?

Aims and Architecture

If the church were to engage missionally and meaningfully with postmodern audiences, then making the effort to understand Derridean deconstruction is about as good a place as any to begin. My aim here is not to survey all of Derrida's voluminous writings, but to focus on relevant aspects of his thought that reflect his evident openness to and conclusions about the possibility of the religious, the divine, the messianic. While the bulk of

---

8. Caputo, *Prayers and Tears of Jacques Derrida*.
9. Derrida, "Circumfession," 154, italics mine.
10. Crockett, "Postmodernism and Its Secrets," 499.

his reflections on religion came rather late in his scholarly life, it is probably incorrect to suggest that Derrida had a change of heart only in his later years about spirituality. It has been suggested, for instance, that as early as the mid-1950s, his master's thesis on Husserl already revealed to an extent the young Derrida's inherent Christian existentialism.[11] One may also recall Derrida quoting, with approval and delight, a statement by Emmanuel Levinas in Derrida's moving eulogy for Levinas on the occasion of the latter's passing in 1995: "You know, one often speaks of ethics to describe what I do, but what really interests me in the end is not ethics, not ethics alone, but the holy, the holiness of the holy (*le saint, la saintete du saint*)."[12] Like Levinas, Derrida, it appeared, was also in search of the holy, and the way he pursued the holy was through a certain "theological" or "spiritual" mode of inquiry which he labeled deconstruction. And if deconstruction had its druthers, it would even claim, indeed it has claimed, that Jesus of Nazareth can rightly be included among the greatest deconstructionists in history.[13] Be that as it may, is deconstruction ultimately hospitable toward Jesus of Nazareth as the Christ?

This book comprises four chapters and a conclusion. Chapter 1 sets the stage for our discussion of Derridean deconstruction by examining how absolutist conceptions of the self—to the extent they serve as a basis and frame for the Christian notion of self—constrain and limit one's spiritual formation, that is, our knowledge of God and our hospitality toward him and his creation. On the other hand, following but also going well beyond Levinas's emphasis on the other, deconstruction's wait for Messiah is predicated upon a fundamental sensitivity to, appreciation for, and hospitality toward heteronomy and otherness, as underscored by deconstruction's pursuit of the *tout autre*, the wholly other. If the God of the Bible is truly our ultimate Other, then any spiritual formation that privileges self over other is but a truncated pilgrimage—a "destination self," so to speak—that leads us not to God but back to ourselves. Chapter 2 seeks to shed light on what deconstruction is or claims to be (by no means an easy task given its apparent inaccessibility for many[14]), paying particular attention to its

---

11. Baring, *Young Derrida and French Philosophy, 1945–1968*. Derrida's master's thesis was subsequently published as *The Problem of Genesis in Husserl's Philosophy*.

12. Derrida, *Adieu to Emmanuel Levinas*, 3.

13. Caputo, *What Would Jesus Deconstruct?*

14. As Derrida once observed, "My most resolute opponents believe that I am too visible, that I am a little too alive, that my name echoes too much in the texts which they nevertheless claim to be inaccessible." Derrida, *Points*, 410.

Introduction

religious implications. The chapter discusses the promises deconstruction heralds—ranging from its affirmation of life to its unremitting dedication to dismantling all forms of idolatry and injustice—and identifies its perils. Granted, they are "perils" from the vantage point of a Christian critique, not least of which is deconstruction's endless wait for the advent of what Richard Kearney terms a "Godless God,"[15] that is, a messiah that ironically, for all of deconstruction's relentless work in demythologization, *awaits fabrication.*

Chapter 3 elaborates on the impossible God of deconstruction, one that remains unknown and nameless because of the indefinite ban imposed by deconstruction on all claims of divine revelation. The concern here over the threat of metaphysical capture is not deconstruction's alone, it is also shared by apophatic/negative theology and its emphasis on God without or beyond "being"—a move which deconstruction nonetheless regards as still too metaphysical because it retains as its key objective the preservation of the preeminence of the Christian God. Secondly and relatedly, despite deconstruction's expressed commitment to agnosticism, aporia, and undecidability—a decision rooted not in the catatonic indecisiveness of Dostoevsky's "underground man,"[16] but in faith as Derrida understood it—it seems that deconstruction, I argue, nonetheless makes a pragmatic choice *against* the biblical Christ. Finally, its devotion to undecidability leads it to the most unexpected of places: notwithstanding its unconditional respect for its wholly other, deconstruction seems to end with the worship of self. But in fairness to deconstruction, we should add this most Derridean of qualifiers: "perhaps!" Chapter 4 furnishes a Christian rejoinder to deconstruction's key objections to Christology, Christian eschatology, and the like. As readers will note, my "dialogue," so-called, with Derrida and deconstruction begins in the first chapter and works its way through the second and third, as we encounter head on deconstruction's significant claims. The case for Christ takes on a more direct and systematic focus in the fourth chapter. While there is much to appreciate and applaud about deconstruction—and how can we not do so when the biblical God takes idolatry and injustice with utmost seriousness—the core bone of contention essentially boils down to this: Deconstructive faith keeps the question of the wholly other alive, whereas biblical faith identifies that other as God

---

15. Kearney, "Desire of God," 124.
16. Dostoevsky, *Notes from Underground.*

and further determines that Christ and he alone is the Messiah. Finally, the book concludes with a summary of its main arguments and key takeaways.

In the interest of self-disclosure, what I present in the following pages, far as my own perspective and position goes, is a view "from the inside"—from within orthodox Christianity, that is.[17] A final minor note: all passages quoted from the Bible below are from the New International Version unless otherwise noted.[18]

---

17. As Gianni Vattimo has described of his perspective and work, "I am an interpreter as long as I am not someone who looks at the world from the outside. I see the external world because I am inside it." Vattimo, "Toward a Nonreligious Christianity," 28.

18. All Scriptures quoted in this book are taken from the Holy Bible, New International Version®, NIV®. Copyright © 1973, 1978, 1984, 2011 by Biblica, Inc.™ Used by permission of Zondervan. All rights reserved worldwide. www.zondervan.com. The "NIV" and "New International Version" are trademarks registered in the United States Patent and Trademark Office by Biblica, Inc.®

1

Self Before Other

Autonomy, Heteronomy, Hospitality

EVERY CHRISTMAS, VERSIONS OF the Nativity scene are played out in churches the world over. The details of the Savior's introduction, from his heavenly abode, into a depraved and inhospitable world two millennia ago are scandalous: the incarnational birth of the Son of God took place in a stable for livestock because there was no room available at the local inn in a Bethlehem swamped with out-of-towners who had returned to their place of origin for the empire-wide census issued by the Roman emperor Caesar Augustus. Shortly thereafter, the Christ (and his earthly parents) would go on the run like fugitives to Egypt to escape Herod's murderous wrath. The concern here has to do with the inhospitality with which one exhibits toward the ultimate Other, God.[1] We recall Christ's invitation to the church

---

1. As the irascible (and hilarious) Luther thundered in a Christmas sermon preached in his final months: "The inn was full. No one would release a room to this pregnant woman. She had to go to a cow stall and there bring forth the Maker of all creatures because nobody would give way. Shame on you, wretched Bethlehem! The inn ought to have been burned with brimstone, for even though Mary had been a beggar maid or unwed, anybody at such a time should have been glad to give her a hand. There are many of you in this congregation who think to yourselves: 'If only I had been there! How quick I would have been to help the baby! I would have washed his linen! How happy I would have been to go with the shepherds to see the Lord lying in the manger!' Yes you would! You say that because you know how great Christ is, but if you had been there at that time you would have done no better than the people of Bethlehem. Childish and silly thoughts are these! Why don't you do it now? You have Christ in your neighbor. You ought to serve him, for what you do to your neighbor in need you do to the Lord Christ himself." Cited

at Laodicea: "Here I am! I stand at the door and knock. If anyone hears my voice and opens the door, I will come in and eat with that person, and they with me" (Rev 3:20). Inhospitality toward Christ happens when his overture is either ignored and the door remains closed. Alternatively, the door may be opened and perhaps greetings are exchanged, but Christ is not invited to enter let alone sup with the occupant. Or Christ finds the place unwelcoming of him, as happened at his hometown of Nazareth where the townsfolk's ostensible familiarity with "Joseph's son" led them to treat Jesus with disdain (Luke 4:14–30). The conditions of inhospitality toward the Messiah may differ depending on context but it happens all the time—even for Christ-followers who are nonetheless given at times, even often, to "grieving the Holy Spirit," as it were (Eph 4:30). When the self is full of itself, there is little room therein to accommodate and to acknowledge alterity, heteronomy, and otherness, much less the absolute and ultimate Other.

The issue of intellectual, individual, and institutional inhospitality, as we shall see in subsequent chapters, was a deep concern for Derrida and informed much of his deconstructive labors. More generally, this concern manifested itself in his work in a variety of ways, not least in his reflections on identity and difference and on the relations between self and other. If, at risk of oversimplifying things, we group views on this matter according, on the one hand, to the proposition that all meaning stems from the self and that all otherness is thereby constituted by the self (let us call this approach "Husserlian") and, on the other hand, the counterproposition that it is in fact the other and otherness that make and shape the self (let us call this "Levinasian"), then it is probably safe to say that the work of Derrida and deconstruction, for the most part, is closer to Emmanuel Levinas's than Edmund Husserl's positions.[2] Given that his conceptual differences with his friend Levinas were debated in the most convivial and even affectionate of ways—quite unlike, say, Derrida's protracted "cold war" with Michel Foucault[3]—others have suggested that latter aspects of Derrida's thinking reflect his move away from the self-other debate toward a quest for openness, plurality, and community.[4] Be that as it may, what binds their respective perspectives is a shared suspicion over totalizing metaphysical

---

in Metaxas, *Martin Luther*, 420.

2. Morin, "Self, The Other, and the Many."
3. Campillo, "Foucault and Derrida."
4. Caputo, "Community without Truth."

narratives—recall postmodernism's incredulity with all Enlightenment-based metanarrative[5]—and their resistance to accepting their inherent indebtedness to heterogeneity and otherness.

My aim here is to set the stage, as it were, for a discussion of Derridean deconstruction and its pursuit of the religious and the messianic, which will occupy the focus in the next two chapters. This chapter will examine how absolutist conceptions of the self—to the extent they serve, if only tacitly, as a basis and frame for the Christian notion of self—constrain and limit one's spiritual formation, that is, our knowledge of God and our hospitality toward him and his creation. If Christian discipleship is understood as "following Jesus to become like Jesus, in order to do what Jesus does,"[6] then the path to Christian maturity is all about Jesus, where, through the course of one's faith pilgrimage, he becomes greater whereas we become less (John 3:30). Yet there can be no lessening of the self without an enlargement of any inherent capacity it might harbor for an intimate knowledge of Christ and generous hospitality toward him. But therein lies the rub: how can the self, one that claims to be already defined and autonomous—or, as we shall see later with deconstruction, one that has so distanced itself from otherness, including the wholly other—ever experience the extent and depth of transformation demanded by radical encounters with Christ, unless and until it relaxes or jettisons certain core suppositions, commitments, and interests that it holds dear, and openly welcomes the other, even God?

Destination Self

Literary aficionados will recall *Cold Mountain*, a historical novel by Charles Frazier which won the U.S. National Book Award for Fiction for 1997. The novel tells the story of W. P. Inman, a wounded deserter from the Confederate Army near the end of the American Civil War who walks for months to return to Ada Monroe, the love of his life, and seeking to heal from the ravages of war by returning home. Arguably, *Cold Mountain* can be read as an allegory about desire and destiny. Partly inspired by Homer's *Odyssey*—both Inman and Odysseus (or Ulysses in the Latin) leave their partners and go off to war; both take a long time and engage in a perilous journey to return home to their loved ones—*Cold Mountain* differs from *Odyssey* in their endings in that Inman dies in Ada's arms whereas Odysseus/Ulysses

---

5. Lyotard, *Postmodern Condition.*
6. Swanson, *Rediscipling the White Church*, 5.

returns safely to his queen Penelope (after passing a series of tests). The concern I have here is not so much with the notion of homecoming, as alluded to in those examples. The purpose of one's quest to understand one's deepest desires is ultimately a journey in self-discovery—or "destination self," as the title of a self-help book has it[7]—which involves a transformative process that either takes one from one place to another or comes full circle. In J. R. R. Tolkien's books, *The Hobbit* and *The Lord of the Rings*, the protagonists of those tales, the hobbits Bilbo Baggins and Frodo Baggins respectively, undertook adventurous journeys—pilgrimages, if you like—with bands of brothers of sorts, during which they matured in wisdom, virtue, and wholeness before returning home to "the Shire." Doubtless, both Baggins' pilgrimages were transformative experiences—mentally, emotionally, spiritually. The same could perhaps be said of Inman or Odysseus, although that is not entirely clear from their respective stories.

That said, what intrigues me about the homecomings in *Cold Mountain* and *Odyssey* is the prospect of reading them as allegories of and statements on self and subjectivity. A journey that begins with the autonomous and unencumbered self typically ends with, well, the self. This is not to imply that such a pilgrimage has neither been eventful, educational, nor, if we must, emancipating. But whatever change the self might have experienced along its way—and by change, I mean the fundamental transformation of one's identity and interests through radical encounters with the ultimate and sovereign other, namely, God—is arguably limited at best.[8] Put differently, the pilgrimage, undertaken on autonomous legs, is likely to find a

---

7. Teurlings, *Destination Self*.

8. The core issue here is human self-centeredness and our inability to overcome it by means other than our being in relationship with the Other, with God. According to Arnold Gehlen in his book *Der Mensch*, humanity's dependence on its environment but also its inability to find ultimate satisfaction in this present world, produces an "indefinite obligation" in humans to seek fulfilment beyond every experience of the world, that is, it generates an openness in humans toward the world and beyond. Neie, *Doctrine of the Atonement*, 105. But as Pannenberg himself argued, this openness in humankind described by Gehlen is opposed by our self-centeredness, which for Pannenberg cannot be successfully resolved by our own efforts, since any progress we could make toward successful resolution of this conflict would play into the hands of our self-centeredness. With no other recourse in conflict resolution other than having our center outside of ourselves, the solution can only be found in God, not the human self, as the true center—a Copernican reorientation of the soul, as it were—who "by warranting the unity of the world as the creator . . . also warrants salvation, that is, the wholeness of our existence in the world, which surmounts the conflict between selfhood and openness to the world." Pannenberg, *Anthropology in Theological Perspective*, 62.

relatively easy resolution because such resolution is ultimately predicated upon the self and its self-inscribed interests. Perhaps we might even say that such a pilgrimage ends up being rather superficial because it gives up far too easily the quest for its deepest desires. "It would seem that Our Lord finds our desires not too strong, but too weak," as C. S. Lewis put it. "We are half-hearted creatures, fooling about with drink and sex and ambition when infinite joy is offered us, like an ignorant child who wants to go on making mud pies in a slum because he cannot imagine what is meant by the offer of a holiday at the sea. We are far too easily pleased."[9] Or, for that matter, disappointed by the limited reach of our search relative to our desires, we lose hope that we will never be able to apprehend and know God who seems too distant and inaccessible. Conversely, some of us may find him too familiar to the point of indifference if not contempt—we irreverently trample his courts (Isa 1:12) as if we are at the mall—because we have lost sight of his holiness. Not unlike the rich young man (in Mark 10:17–31) who sought eternal life but walked away emptyhanded, so disillusioned was he by Jesus's seemingly impossible requirement that stood at odds with the man's self-interest—and tragically missing the all-important fact that the Lord "looked at him and loved him" (Mark 10:21)—we risk giving up on and abandoning the quest altogether because, fixated as we are on privileging the self, we either steadfastly refuse to radically accommodate otherness or we do not know how to welcome much less embrace otherness, even if the other were God himself.

Transaction and Transcendence Overdone?

A religious pilgrimage that begins with a self already defined and resistant to otherness is more likely than not to be grounded in various forms of Baalism—even if it is undertaken with spiritual formation and Christlike maturity as its ostensible intent.[10] Since the self is treated as an already given and self-evident as an autonomous actor, it ends up objectifying and reifying not only the self but other subjectivities with which the self subsequently interacts, including God.[11] Objectification and reification are processes by which the self and other are treated as objects rather than subjects. It involves an amnesia of sorts regarding the social context within which

---

9. Lewis, *Weight of Glory, and Other Addresses*, 26.
10. Peterson, *Five Smooth Stones for Pastoral Work*.
11. Nussbaum, "Objectification."

self-other interact and the possibilities for mutual constitution within such a relationship.¹² The notion of two given autonomous subjects interacting with one another would seem to proffer little room for change or, for that matter, meaningful knowledge. By contrast, think, if you will, of the exchange between God and Abraham, where Abraham pleads with the Lord on behalf of the proverbial sin city of Sodom (Gen 18:16–23), or that with Moses, where Moses pleads with God on behalf of the Israelites who had engaged in idolatry (Exod 32:7–14). Without getting into the thorny question of "whether God changes his mind," in both instances the text suggests God seemingly tweaking his initial propositions in response to the intercessions of his servants. Both instances involved interactions undertaken in heteronomous covenantal relationships between Maker and men that are not inscribed within the logic of autonomous subjectivity.

To be sure, when we treat and relate with another in an objectifying fashion, a certain knowledge about that other is produced as a result. When conducted in that vein, the process of knowledge constitution—as Edward Said, following Foucault, might put it—can be understood as a practice for managing, and thereby constructing, otherness through issuing statements about it, sanctioning views of it, describing and teaching it, settling and domesticating it, and ultimately policing it.¹³ Perhaps, like Susan Pevensie worrying over whether the lion Aslan is safe to deal with in Lewis's *The Lion, the Witch and the Wardrobe*, we would rather relate with others that we consider safe, and as such we engage in domestication to ensure that that is indeed the case—even if it means downplaying or even denying those others their "natures," as it were. As Derrida once put it, "Monsters cannot be announced. One cannot say: 'Here are our monsters,' without immediately turning the monsters into pets."¹⁴ Perhaps, not unlike a scientist might, we view and study our others with cool detachment or an exaggerated intimacy without really relating meaningfully with them. "The other person is not simply a step on the philosopher's ladder to metaphysical truth," as Simon Critchley has urged. "And perhaps the true source of wonder with which, as Aristotle claimed, philosophy begins, is not to be found by staring into the starry heavens, but by looking into another's eyes, for here is a palpable infinity that can never exhaust one's curiosity."¹⁵ Objectification

---

12. Lijster, "'All Reification Is a Forgetting.'"
13. Said, *Orientalism*.
14. Derrida, "Some Statements and Truisms about Neologisms," 80.
15. Critchley, "Introduction," 27.

leads to two problems that hinder our spiritual formation. On the one hand, it encourages a relationship with God that is primarily transactional in kind and grounded by a strict expectation of mutual reciprocity; on the other hand, it encourages an overly high view of God—granted, God is way higher than the highest heavens! (Job 11:7–8)—and exaggerates his transcendence to the point he is inaccessible.

Let us start with the transactional. Reverence for God is rendered on the expectation that he blesses and prospers us in return. Granted, there is no getting away from this aspect in our relationship with God. As the patriarch Jacob prayed what appears to be a vow of conditional compliance following his dream encounter with the God of his fathers at Luz/Bethel: "Then Jacob made a vow, saying, 'If God will be with me and will watch over me on this journey I am taking and will give me food to eat and clothes to wear so that I return safely to my father's household, then the LORD will be my God and this stone that I have set up as a pillar will be God's house, and of all that you give me I will give you a tenth'" (Gen 28:20–22). Indeed, mutual reciprocity is a fundamental basis of familial and societal relations; it serves, if you will, as the basis of the social contract. Contractarian theory holds that people are primarily self-interested and rational actors. As such, rational assessments would lead them to conclude that the maximization of their self-interest causes them to act morally toward one another and to consent to governmental authority. Contractarians argue on utilitarian or consequentialist grounds that we each are motivated to accept morality first because, as Hobbes famously argued, we are vulnerable to the depredations of others, and second because we can all benefit from cooperation with others.[16] For Hobbes, the social contract is predicated upon a mutuality of interest, which causes people to consensually transfer their right to the sovereign.[17] Indeed, the assumption of mutual reciprocity is central to Hobbes's understanding of contract because, for him, the grounding of obligation in civil society is in fact the principle of reciprocity.[18] The reciprocity principle is equally at the heart of the liberal face of social contract theory, namely, contractualism. It takes inspiration from Kant's insight that we ought to treat persons not as means but always as ends in themselves. Kant understood morality and responsibility as a reasonable and rational act of an autonomous will and an application of the golden rule: "treat

---

16. Narveson, *Libertarian Idea*, 148.
17. Hobbes, *Leviathan*.
18. Dore, "Deconstructing and Reconstructing Hobbes," 853.

others how you wish to be treated," or "do unto others as you would have them do unto you."[19] For Kant, the motivation for acting hospitably toward another ultimately stems from self-interest; the desire that likewise one will receive hospitality in return. Grounded as such on the equal moral status of persons, contractual theory offers an account of the authority of moral standards and what constitutes rightness and wrongness.[20] The version propounded by John Rawls emphasizes principles to which everyone could agree.[21] Its assumed sociality also raises interesting questions about the place of mutuality and reciprocity in any relationship between self and other. Crucially, what is at hand here is not mutuality and reciprocity broadly defined, but as they are conceived and expressed through the lens of an autonomous and transactional subjectivity, as we shall see below.

Although they are neither identical nor interchangeable, there is however no denying the robust link between reciprocity and transactionalism. But where the assumption and expectation of reciprocity is given pride of place over all else, it risks turning our relationship with God into something that is purely transactional, calculative, and even commodified. "On the one hand, if someone does something nice for me in the reciprocal community, I want to give back, therefore creating more value for the group and further incentivizing people to contribute. That's great," as Fabian Pfortmüller has mused. "On the other hand, if I give and contribute, I expect something in return. And what if that doesn't happen? And that's where reciprocity becomes a slippery slope, because it encourages transactional behavior, not long-term relationship building."[22] Indeed, the way we treat the things that matter to God—truth, mercy, justice, etc.—also risks becoming a matter of transaction and calculation, possibly even commodification. As Derrida insisted, justice toward the other is always unequal, incalculable, and irreducible to law because justice, as Levinas said, is precisely one's relation to the other.[23] The point here is neither to knock reciprocity and transaction nor dismiss them altogether. For instance, the practice of the exchange of gifts is grounded in our conception of mutual obligation and reciprocity; it establishes a moral bond enabling the functioning of societies and forms a

19. Willaschek, "Right and Coercion."
20. Scanlon, *What We Owe to Each Other*.
21. Rawls, "Kantian Constructivism in Moral Theory."
22. Pfortmüller, "Why Communities Based on Reciprocity are Selling Themselves Short."
23. Derrida, *Deconstruction in a Nutshell*, 17–18.

key dimension of the social contract.[24] However, any exercise in hospitality and gift-giving that is kept strictly within the closed framework of exchange and reciprocity—to the point where, as Pfortmüller might say, it becomes purely transactional—risks losing the very qualities that make a gift what it is; at that point, it ceases to be a gift and instead becomes a commodity. As we shall see again and again in the subsequent chapters, a gift, for Derrida, is without limit and measure, it is excessive and it overruns its borders, so to speak.[25]

The objectification of self and of God can also lead to the perception that God is overly transcendental—so physically, socially, and morally distanced from his creation—to the point that it excludes the possibility that God is also immanent. The idea of God as transcendent is central to theism and is rooted in the idea of the holy[26]—the "innermost core" of all religious belief, as Rudolf Otto observed.[27] But nowhere is the holiness of God more emphasized than in the Judeo-Christian faith. As R. C. Sproul, commenting on Isa 6, once observed, "The Bible says that God is holy, holy, holy. Not that He is merely holy, or even holy, holy. He is holy, holy, holy. The Bible never says that God is love, love, love, or mercy, mercy, mercy, or wrath, wrath, wrath, or justice, justice, justice. It does say that He is holy, holy, holy, the whole earth is full of His glory."[28] Another crucial aspect of divine transcendence, tied to the holiness of God, is that of otherness and separation, of something that is marked off or set apart. To cite Sproul again: "When the Bible calls God holy it means primarily that God is transcendentally separate. He is so far above and beyond us that He seems almost totally foreign to us. To be holy is to be 'other,' to be different in a special way. The same basic meaning is used when the word holy is applied to earthly things."[29] The holiness of God is not the only thing that sets him apart from creation; he is different than his creation in so many ways. "'For my thoughts are not your thoughts, neither are your ways my ways,' declares the LORD. 'As the heavens are higher than the earth, so are my ways higher than your ways and my thoughts than your thoughts'" (Isa 55:8–9). In other words, the otherness of God is not just any otherness; it

24. Mauss, *Gift*.
25. Derrida, *Given Time*, 91.
26. Hudson, "Concept of Divine Transcendence."
27. Otto, *Idea of the Holy*, 20.
28. Sproul, *Holiness of God*, 40.
29. Sproul, *Holiness of God*, 55.

is, as Otto insisted, an otherness that is verbally indefinable. We may recall Thomistic arguments to the effect that God cannot be defined in the strict sense of define, for to be defined is to be limited.[30] God the numinous Presence is the *mysterium*, the enigmatic wholly other who is entirely different from anything we experience in ordinary life, the *tremendum* that provokes awe and terror because it is an overwhelming power, as well as, at the same time, the *fascinans* that is full of mercy and grace.[31] God is neither the most powerful individual being nor is he the greatest conceivable being; put simply, he is being itself.[32] I will return to this apophatic understanding of God in subsequent chapters.

Divine transcendence does not negate divine immanence; the two are not mutually exclusive but mutually determine one another.[33] For Levinas, the call of the other and our response to it connotes immanence because they principally involve "face-to-face" encounters. Or as another scholar has put it, "We are living in the face of the other, seeking or fleeing it, running the risk of losing our own face."[34] As Derrida once argued:

> We should stop thinking about God as someone, over there, way up there, transcendent, and, what is more—into the bargain, precisely—capable, more than any satellite orbiting in space, of seeing into the most secret of the most interior places. It is perhaps necessary, if we are to follow the traditional Judeo-Christiano-Islamic injunction, but also at the risk of turning it against that tradition, to think of God and of the name of God without such idolatrous stereotyping or representation. Then we might say: God is the name of the possibility I have of keeping a secret that is visible from the interior but not from the exterior.[35]

The face-to-face relationship is what constitutes a metaphysical condition for Levinas because it is before all things; it is certainly ontologically prior to philosophy and theology.[36] The Christmas season is a constant reminder of the notion of God becoming immanent in the world by self-incarnation: Immanuel, God with us (Matt 1:23). The notion of immanence

---

30. Spencer, "Defense of the Metaphysics of Divine Simplicity," 3.
31. Otto, *Idea of the Holy*.
32. Spencer, "Defense of the Metaphysics of Divine Simplicity," 4–5.
33. Kim, "Transcendence and Immanence."
34. Waldenfels, "Levinas and the Face of the Other," 65.
35. Derrida, *Gift of Death*, 108.
36. Levinas, *Totality and Infinity*, 84.

continues even after Christ's resurrection. The conferring of his Spirit to his body of believers suggests the possibility of a permanent divine immanence—as Paul admonished the Corinthian believers, "Don't you know that you yourselves are God's temple and that God's Spirit dwells in your midst?" (1 Cor 3:16)—albeit one that could be limited by sin and man's grieving of the Spirit (Eph 4:30). But divine immanence—or the presence and working of the Holy Spirit, for that matter—are not just New Testament realities. As King David, who insisted that, "The Lord is close to the brokenhearted" (Ps 34:18a), also conceded in another place: "Where can I go from your Spirit? Where can I flee from your presence? If I go up to the heavens, you are there; if I make my bed in the depths, you are there. If I rise on the wings of the dawn, if I settle on the far side of the sea, even there your hand will guide me, your right hand will hold me fast" (Ps 139:7–10). But as we shall see in the subsequent chapters, divine immanence and immediacy as understood here is not quite the same thing as deconstruction's logic of secret interiorization Derrida described above.

What might a faith that eschews those extremes look like? Blameless and upright Job's declaration in response to untold and unfathomable personal loss and devastation belied Satan's erroneous assumption that Job's worship of God was purely transactional in motivation: "Naked I came from my mother's womb, and naked I will depart. The Lord gave and the Lord has taken away; may the name of the Lord be praised" (Job 1:21). But neither did Job see God as overly transcendent. Granted, Job might have felt that God had become remote and inaccessible as he (Job) languished in his sorrowful state, wrongly accused by his friends of having sinned and thereby in need of repentance. Remarkably, Job's defense was built around his resolute belief that not only was his God-given righteousness intact, but that his hope of seeing God with his own eyes would be fulfilled (Job 19:27). For example, Mike Mason has made the following observation about Job's unwavering trust in God under extremely difficult circumstances:

> Under attack Job groaned, he wailed, he doubted and fell into deep depression, he lashed out like an infuriated animal—and yes, he even sinned. Yet when it came to this one point regarding the settled fact of his status of irreproachable blamelessness before the Lord, he refused to give an inch. Having placed his trust totally in God, he violently resisted the notion that there might still be some other step he should take, something else he must "do," to gain God's favor under adverse circumstances. Like Abraham, "against

all hope, [he] in hope believed" (Rom. 4:18). In short, he had 'the righteousness that comes from God and is by faith' (Phil. 3:9).[37]

This assuredly is not the desire of a man for whom the immanence of God was a foreign notion. And Job was rewarded for his faith when, from Job 38 on, God finally "drew near" and spoke and terrified him into silence—presumably not in the gentle whisper with which God spoke with Elijah at Horeb (1 Kgs 19:12)! And the consequence of all of that was a self radically transformed via a powerful encounter with the living God, the ultimate other: "My ears had heard of you but now my eyes have seen you. Therefore I despise myself and repent in dust and ashes" (Job 42:5–6).

Other Before Self

A key reason why we may be missing out on God's larger purposes, I suggest, could be due to a philosophical blindness to God as other that cannot, that must not, be subject to our self-serving efforts to domesticate him. Yet this could well be the indirect consequence of an ontological absolutism that resists and refuses any logic other than that based on an autonomous freedom, which renders it impervious to the possibility that subjectivity is always and already interdependent and hence heteronomous.[38] Understandably, it is not immediately apparent why the postmodern critique matters if at all to how Christians understand the formation of the self. The development of Christianity in the early modern West—and certainly in the United States—included a longstanding series of battles and accommodations with Enlightenment ideals, leading to the emergence, inter alia, of liberal Protestantism.[39] But it is not just the self-declared liberal facets of Christianity that are in question here. With the widespread infusion of scientistic and humanistic influences into the Church at large, a major consequence has not only been the relegation of biblical truth from the pride of place it once enjoyed, but equally the Hellenization and secularization of our understanding and practice of the Word of God.[40]

---

37. Mason, *Gospel According to Job*, 22.
38. Levinas and Kearney, "Dialogue with Emmanuel Levinas," 20.
39. Marsden, *Soul of the American University*.
40. Moreland, *Scientism and Secularism*.

Self Before Other
The Autonomous Self in Liberalism and Conservatism

Liberalism advances the notion of unencumbered selves that are at once individualist in asserting the moral primacy of the individual over any social collective, egalitarian in granting to all the same moral status whilst denying any rank ordering of differences in moral worth among human beings, universalist in affirming the moral unity of all humans and relegating their specific historical and cultural associations, and meliorist (i.e., the metaphysical belief that progress is a real concept leading to an improvement of the world) in affirming "the corrigibility and improvability of all social institutions and political arrangements."[41] Grand and ambitious, perhaps even utopian, the liberal agenda has a lot of good things in it, not least the embrace of hospitality. As even the conservative thinker and former president of the American Enterprise Institute, Arthur C. Brooks, has allowed, "Welcoming the stranger is one of the great moral traditions liberals have."[42] However, liberalism's insistence on self-autonomy—to ultimately place self before all others, if you like—is plausibly a huge stumbling block against the pursuit of the knowledge of God. The concern here is not that liberalism lacks consideration for others—a rather absurd claim given what has just been said about it. Rather, it is its neglect of heteronomy, and the ramifications of that neglect for the political, social, and religious implications for the self, that is of foremost concern here.

But it is important to clarify at the out-start that the assumption of autonomy is not unique to liberalism; it is equally an accepted supposition in conservative thought or, to be specific, in laissez-faire conservatism as opposed to, say, status quo conservatism and social conservatism.[43] That said, even in the case of social conservatism—which some equate with authoritarianism, fairly or otherwise—its communitarian aspect betrays a collective and even totalitarian self, where a collective and no less sovereign identity replaces the individual self of laissez-fare conservatism.[44] Irving Kristol, regarded by many as the founder of the contemporary neoconservative movement in the United States, once insisted that what is inherently wrong with liberalism is in fact liberalism itself, which in his view consists in "a metaphysics and a mythology that is woefully blind to human and

---

41. Gray, *Liberalism*, xii.
42. Brooks, "Don't Shun Conservative Professors."
43. Stenner, "Three Kinds of 'Conservatism.'"
44. Stenner, "Three Kinds of 'Conservatism.'"

political reality."[45] To the extent that aspects of conservative thought also share in the supposition of autonomous and unencumbered subjectivities as its starting point, Kristol's critique of liberalism could equally be applied to conservatism as well. Bearing in mind this broader understanding is important as we continue.

Heteronomy Before Autonomy

A useful guide to the critique of autonomy is the Jewish-French philosopher and Talmudic scholar Emmanuel Levinas, whose ideas served as both inspiration as well as a point of departure for Derrida's deconstruction. Whether Levinas's ideas can be rightly considered postmodern is a hotly debated issue,[46] but what is undeniable is the impact they had on Derrida's own thinking in intellectual and philosophical, but crucially ethical and arguably even spiritual terms—in the sense of a fundamental appreciation for and responsibility to the divine. According to Levinas, the self is heteronomous *before* it is autonomous,[47] which presumably implies that no subject is ever truly autonomous as the context and condition of its emergence is always and already one of heteronomy and interdependence. Some find this idea of an ethical relation with the other that exists prior to knowledge to be challenging because it lacks the proper place of reflection for moral philosophy, more traditionally conceived.[48] But as we shall see in subsequent chapters, Derrida's critique of the metaphysics of God and the knowability of the Messiah for which deconstruction (endlessly) awaits is tied precisely to this notion, whose implications are fundamental to the understanding of *homo religiosus*. As Derrida once explained regarding Jan Patočka's conception of religion in terms of the self and its relationship with otherness:

> The genesis of responsibility that Patočka proposes will not simply describe a history of religion or religiousness. It will be combined with a genealogy of the subject who says 'myself,' the subject's relation to itself as an instance of liberty, singularity, and responsibility, the relation to self as being before the other: the other in its relation to infinite alterity, one who regards without being seen but

45. Cited in Murray, *Neoconservatism*, 45.
46. Alford, "Bauman and Levinas."
47. Morgan, *Cambridge Introduction to Emmanuel Levinas*, 114.
48. Westphal, "Of God who comes to mind, by Emmanuel Levinas," 524.

also whose infinite goodness *gives* in an experience that amounts to a *gift of death [donner la mort]*.⁴⁹

Clearly, this is *not* where the autonomous self is at. Much as people and things risk becoming objectified through processes that treat them as such, the same risk confronts Christian conceptions of the self so long as they are beholden, if only indirectly, to the economistic logics behind liberal subjectivity. But it is not only the human self that is at issue here; as we saw in the preceding section, we are equally adept at objectifying God whether through treating our relationship with Him in overly transactional and/or transcendental ways. As Derrida once observed about the pervasive concern behind Levinas's scholarship, "The complicity of theoretical objectivity and mystical communion will be Levinas's true target."⁵⁰ Thus understood, ethical systems that rely on totalized foundations, as does liberalism (and possibly Enlightened-based conceptions of conservatism as well), are likely to fail. Indeed, it was the liberalism of his day that indirectly paved the way for the Nazi regime to emerge in interwar Germany, while offering precious little by way of its opposition.⁵¹ After all, it was the Weimar Republic, arguably one of the most liberal states in history, which overwhelmingly passed the infamous Enabling Law that granted the Reich chancellor, Adolf Hitler, the power to enact legislation without prior consent of the German parliament.⁵² If anything, Levinas advocated the denouncement of liberalism because he saw it as "insufficiently human" because of its inconsideration of alterity and otherness.⁵³ Not surprisingly, he has been criticized by liberal scholars as "antihuman" for having raised such a scandalous charge against liberalism. But it may be argued that his so-called antihumanism is neither

---

49. Derrida, *Gift of Death*, 3, italics original.
50. Derrida, "Violence and Metaphysics," 87.
51. Levinas and Hand, "Reflections on the Philosophy of Hitlerism," 63.
52. Kurlander, *Living with Hitler*. Recent worries over a potential "authoritarian turn" in the United States have the Weimar Republic in mind. In view of the Capitol Hill riot in January 2021, liberal activists are concerned over potential "nightmare scenarios" for future sessions of the U.S. Congress, with many referring to the prospect of a "Weimar moment"—with visions of a bloodless conservative coup in the state capitols endorsed by conservative courts and culminating in a decisive vote for Trump-supporting Republicans in Congress. "Our democracy is in great peril today," according to Norm Eisen, a prominent Democratic lawyer who co-founded the nonpartisan States United Democracy Center. "We're in a Weimar moment in America." Cited in Berman, "Kamala Harris Might Have to Stop the Steal."
53. Levinas, *Otherwise Than Being or Beyond Essence*, 127.

inhuman nor inhumane because, rather than eradicating the human, it liberates liberalism from its myopia to the fact that human communities, as Paul Kahn has persuasively demonstrated, do not function solely based on legal rationality but are equally bound together by faith, love, and identity.[54] According to Levinas, the notion of modern antihumanism better approximates what it means to be human than its liberal counterpart does because, by embracing things like sacrifice, submission, and humility as key to the human condition, antihumanism in fact humanizes as it "clears the place (*il fait place nette*) for subjectivity positing itself in abnegation, in sacrifice, in a substitution which precedes the will."[55] Take, for example, the following biblical passages that prioritize those very themes:

> Then Jesus said to his disciples, "Whoever wants to be my disciple must deny themselves and take up their cross and follow me. For whoever wants to save their life will lose it, but whoever loses their life for me will find it" (Matt 16:24–25).
>
> "Abba, Father," he said, "everything is possible for you. Take this cup from me. Yet not what I will, but what you will" (Mark 14:36).
>
> The bride belongs to the bridegroom. The friend who attends the bridegroom waits and listens for him, and is full of joy when he hears the bridegroom's voice. That joy is mine, and it is now complete. He must become greater; I must become less (John 3:29–30).
>
> My command is this: Love each other as I have loved you. Greater love has no one than this: to lay down one's life for one's friends. You are my friends if you do what I command (John 15:12–14).

Or, in the words of Miroslav Volf and Matthew Croasmun, "It requires a death of the self and its rising again and a resultant shift in seeing and hearing, *a new set of eyes and ears as the organs of a new self.*"[56] If what Levinas was indeed calling for is a subjectivity that precedes the will and waives its rights in voluntary abnegation and sacrifice, then it begs the question whether the aforementioned Scriptures can allow let alone accommodate an autonomous subjectivity. As Kahn has argued, the blindness of liberalism (and, we might add, conservatism) to sacrifice—after all, the contract is the all-important element in liberal thought—renders it incapable of understanding, let alone explain, how the modern state has given us the

---

54. Kahn, *Putting Liberalism in Its Place*.
55. Cited in Oksala, *Foucault on Freedom*, 205.
56. Volf and Croasmun, *For the Life of the World*, 118, italics original.

rule of law while also bringing us to the brink of nuclear annihilation.[57] Indeed, as Schopenhauer or, for that matter, Nietzsche have reminded us, a world absent sacrificial love leaves us not with the enlightened rationality presupposed by the Enlightenment but, more likely, a world comprised of wills trapped in struggles over power and survival.[58]

Going for Broke

As we have seen, both the transactional and transcendental ripostes resist going far and deep in the quest for the Other, to be fully abandoned to it. As Augustine put it in the opening paragraph of *The Confessions*, "You stir man to take pleasure in praising you, because you have made us for yourself, and our heart is restless until it rests in you." Augustine's express restlessness implied a readiness on his part to go to the uttermost parts of the universe to seek for rest that could only be found in his God. The inference that some have sought to draw from this passage is that a true quest for one's deepest desires and their satisfaction, as defined by Christ and not oneself, must necessarily go "all the way," that is, complete abandonment in and to God; the evangelical archetype of this sort of abandonment to God is perhaps that found in the popular devotional *My Utmost for His Highest* by Oswald Chambers, the Scottish Baptist and Holiness Movement evangelist and teacher. The biblical picture that comes to mind is that of Ezekiel's vision of his incremental immersion in the river—the "river of God," as it were, that flows from God's temple—at progressively deeper depths until the water levels are well over the prophet's head, and he is literally abandoned to God (Ezek 47:3–5). The refusal to do so does not necessarily mean a resistance to entering the kingdom of God. It signals a contentment, arising either from spiritual lassitude or obstruction or fear, to merely linger at the outer courts rather than seizing the divine invitation to enter "the Most Holy Place"—to draw near(er) to God, as it were (Heb 10:19–22). Or, as Charles Spurgeon reportedly averred, "Some Christians sail their boat in such low spiritual waters that the keel scrapes on the gravel all the way to Heaven, instead of being carried on a floodtide."[59] And yet if folks in such a middling estate are among those whom Christ considers neither hot nor cold

---

57. Kahn, *Putting Liberalism in Its Place*.
58. Nietzsche, *Will to Power*, and Schopenhauer, *World as Will and Representation*.
59. Bonnke, *Evangelism by Fire*, 119.

but lukewarm, then the prospect that they may be spat out of his mouth is surely discomforting (Rev 3:16).

Be that as it may, the premature curtailment of one's quest for desire and destiny[60]—that one thing which we ask from the Lord and that only which we seek, as David said (Ps 27:4)—when too easily satiated by contentment with second best, could lead to one missing out on the "bigger dreams" that God may wish to realize in and through us. "When I've waited on the Lord, that's when He has delighted me by fulfilling far bigger dreams," as the Christian entrepreneur Terry Looper has intimated. "In one instance, I'd been carrying a desire around for half my life. And in that dream come true, I learned what I would have forfeited had I settled for the lesser desire that preceded it."[61] Clearly, the kind of quest alluded to by Looper, Augustine, and Lewis is not the sort easily satisfied with what second best—the lesser good, or mud pies in the slum to which half-hearted or prematurely truncated journeys in self-discovery lead, where the search for self brings more of the same—can muster and deliver. As Augustine reportedly taught in a sermon, "If you believe what you like in the Gospel, and reject what you don't like, it is not the Gospel you believe, but yourself." The search for self that begins with the self inevitably begets and ends with the same old self—literally, *destination self*. But as we shall see in the following chapters, even the relentless pursuit of otherness, one as single-mindedly dedicated as Derridean deconstruction in its quest for the holy and the messianic—the so-called "wholly other" (*tout autre*) and the impossible God of which nothing can be known or revealed—is no guarantee that one would not end up back at home base, a destination self, rather than a transformed/transforming identity that finds its true homecoming in Christ and he alone. And that simply is not good enough.

---

60. Ganssle, *Our Deepest Desires*.

61. Looper, *Sacred Pace*. Looper goes on in that same book to say, "Part of my responsibility is to turn a deaf ear to the often-tempting things my flesh says will bring me satisfaction, and instead wait on the Lord for the desires of my heart. I live in complete confidence that as I operate from the heart, God will work all things for my good, my better, and my best. He said so! He will be good to me—delighting me beyond anything I could ever ask for or imagine, never making me settle for second best."

2

Deconstruction's Promises (and Perils)

> I don't care to argue that Derrida is right—what good philosopher would ever characterize his work as right? Philosophy is a way of exercising the mind, of keeping it from becoming complacent. It urges us to think long and hard about things, to make ourselves uncomfortable, to question our very existence, and to work to improve ourselves, and the world, through rigorous examination. What I learned from Jacques Derrida was simply to examine everything in the most fundamental way. I think differently about the hour I spent with the unfailingly polite man with the simple life. I had read him as a polite, charming man with a complicated philosophy and a simple life. In retrospect, I realize that he was consistent, the man I sat down with was Derrida as I first encountered him in text: a dark horse, a sly old fox.[1]

> Many otherwise unmalicious people have in fact been guilty of wishing for deconstruction's demise—if only to relieve themselves of the burden of trying to understand it.[2]

IN HIS 1993 BOOK eponymously titled *Jacques Derrida*—which consisted in his co-author Geoffrey Bennington's attempt to give an "authoritative account" of Derrida's theory and method of deconstruction, on the one hand, and Derrida's own effort at deconstructing Bennington's reading of him and his work on the other—Derrida shocked his disciples and detractors alike with the seemingly casual but no doubt thoroughly deliberate statement that his prodigious oeuvre had been "read less and less well

1. Dilday, "Jacques Derrida."
2. Stephens, "Jacques Derrida."

over almost twenty years, *like my religion about which nobody understands anything.*"³ Derrida continued with the revelation that his own mother, rather than approaching him directly, had instead asked others whether her son (Derrida) still believed in God; to this, Derrida, perhaps with a touch of indignation, insisted that his mother "must have known that the constancy of God in my life is called by other names, so that I quite rightly pass for an atheist, the omnipresence to me of what I call God in my absolved, absolutely private language . . ."⁴

Far as the world of continental philosophy went, Derrida's confession was earthshattering, the intellectual equivalent of a megaton nuclear explosion going off. What, the valiant champion and indefatigable standard bearer of deconstruction and an avowed atheist to boot, not only "outing" himself as a person of faith but revealing that the prime motivation behind his decades-long deconstructive enterprise had all along been *religious* in nature?⁵ Naturally, not everyone approved of such a revelation; for example, Derrida's good friend Jean-Luc Nancy once warned that the philosophical turn to religion is dangerous because, fairly or otherwise, it implies (in Nancy's view) a kind of disease, it belongs to the province of the gullible, it is akin to fascism, and it smacks of political correctness.⁶ But Derrida, it turns out, had been waiting all along for the coming of Messiah—just not the messiahs haloed by the world's orthodox religions or what Derrida termed "concrete messianisms."⁷ In the subsequent flurry of attempts by scholars to reinterpret Derrida and deconstruction in the light of their purported religious inclinations, John D. Caputo, perhaps Derrida's most sympathetic and eloquent apologist, explained that deconstruction "is not out to undo God or deny faith, or to mock science or make nonsense out of literature, or to break the law or, generally, to ruin any of those hoary

---

3. Derrida, "Circumfession," 154, italics mine.

4. Derrida, "Circumfession," 155.

5. Commenting on his lifelong distrust of orthodox religion, Derrida reminisced about his Sephardic Jewish upbringing in El Biar in French-ruled Algeria: "I started resisting religion as a young adolescent, not in the name of atheism, but I found religion as it was practiced within my family to be fraught with misunderstanding. It struck me as thoughtless, just blind repetitions, and there was one thing in particular I found unacceptable: that was the way honors were dispersed. The honor of carrying and reading the Torah was auctioned off in the synagogue, and I found that terrible." Cited in Peeters, *Derrida*, 21.

6. Nancy, *Dis-Enclosure*.

7. Derrida, *Specters of Marx*, 59.

things at whose very mention all your muscles constrict," but is in fact in the business of saving them—including, it would seem, Christianity—from all metaphysical conceits and political acts of domestication and control imposed on them by men and institutions, with usually good intentions but often disastrous consequences.[8] Moreover, deconstruction has its eye fixed resolutely on justice—if such a thing exists, as Derrida often qualified—because the very essence of deconstruction, as Derrida insisted, *is* justice.[9] Whether and how this is the case is what I aim to explore in this chapter.

What is Deconstruction?

> The very idea of a Messiah who is never to show and whom we accordingly desire all the more is the very paradigm of deconstruction . . . The impossibility is not the doom and gloom of deconstruction; it is not an end but a beginning, for *we begin by the impossible*. Indeed the end would only come if the Messiah were actually to show up, for what would then be left to hope for?[10]

Some introductory thoughts on deconstruction are in order. As Paul de Man once observed, deconstruction has either been dismissed as a harmless parlor game or denounced as a terrorist weapon.[11] Neither of these views is particularly helpful. For that matter, even sympathetic readings that reduce deconstruction to a rank determinism and monism of "nothing outside the text" understandings do a disservice to deconstruction—even though Derrida is most associated with that very phrase[12]—for the simple reason that their reasoning leads them into self-imposed philosophical traps where, more likely than not, they are caught within narrating themselves. What can be said about deconstruction—using the terms of modernity, no less—is that it aims to be a kind of "new enlightenment" that brings a near-impossible level of unremitting vigilance and heightened scrutiny to anything this side of Heaven that promotes and presents itself as essence or presence or being—truth, tradition, ethics, democracy, justice, God. At the same time, in believing in the possibility for the untainted purity of such

---

8. Caputo, *Prayers and Tears of Jacques Derrida*, 5.
9. Derrida, "Force of Law," 15, and Caputo, "Hyperbolic Justice."
10. Caputo, "Apostles of the Impossible," 186, italics original.
11. Norris, *Deconstruction*, xii.
12. Derrida, *Of Grammatology*, 159.

things, Derrida, it could be said, was in fact a true child of the Enlightenment whose relentless skepticism laid bare the hypocritical dogmatism of self-styled guardians of the Enlightenment whose words and deeds nonetheless betrayed its spirit, so to speak.[13] In Derrida's words: "What I call 'deconstruction,' even when it is directed toward something from Europe, is European; it is a product of Europe, a relation of Europe to itself as an experience of radical alterity. Since the time of the Enlightenment, Europe has undertaken a perpetual self-critique, and in this perfectible heritage there is a chance for a future. At least I would like to hope so, and that is what feeds my indignation when I hear people definitively condemning Europe as if it were but the scene of its crimes."[14] To refer to deconstruction as a philosophy may be pushing it; Derrida famously had a torrid time with analytic philosophers who rejected his efforts as other than philosophy—as argued by the group of philosophers in protest of the University of Cambridge's decision to grant Derrida an honorary degree in 1992—due in no small part to his style, which was frequently more literary than philosophical and therefore more evocative than argumentative.

At risk of oversimplification, many modernist renditions of truth, justice, and the like tend to assume a teleology and provide maps and blueprints pointing and fixing the way to their realization. On the other hand, deconstruction, which Derrida insisted is eschatological in orientation given its longing for the messianic,[15] "issues a warning that the road ahead is still under construction, that there is blasting and the danger of falling rock."[16] This is accomplished not through the application of a method or tool to a specific statement or event under interrogation from the outside because—and here is its important contribution—deconstruction is something that happens *within* texts and traditions, giving rise to new interpretations and unexpected twists.[17] Deconstruction does not seek to wantonly destroy and annihilate but, in Caputo's words, "to loosen and unlock structures, to let the shock of alterity set them in motion, to allow them to function more freely and inventively, to produce new forms, and

---

13. Arguably, the same could be said here of Nietzsche, meaning, that he too remained a progeny of Enlightenment despite—or because of—his relentless and devastating critique of it. Garrard, "Nietzsche for and against the Enlightenment."

14. Derrida, *Learning to Live Finally*, 44–45.

15. Derrida, *Specters of Marx*, 44–45.

16. Caputo, *Against Ethics*, 4.

17. Caputo, *Prayers and Tears of Jacques Derrida*, 9.

above all to say yes, *oui, oui*, to something whose coming eye hath not seen nor ear heard."[18] Deconstruction furnishes insights into the systematic and structural nature of signification combined with a rejection of—or at least a persistent resistance to—the metaphysical closure of those structures.[19] And if metaphysical closure is an airtight compartment hermetically sealed to prevent any questioning let alone criticism of what it protects and preserves, then to deconstruct is to keep thought, or the possibility of it, alive. "If I understand deconstruction, deconstruction is not an exposure of error, certainly not other people's error," as Gayatri Chakravorty Spivak explained. "The critique in deconstruction, the most serious critique in deconstruction, is the critique of something that is extremely useful, something without which we cannot do anything."[20] Far from a random or indifferent gesture, deconstruction calls attention to institutions that regularize and normalize everything from literature to democracy and exposes them to the otherness that is always and already residing on the margins of texts and traditions.[21] Deconstruction accomplishes this from *within* those texts and traditions in situated, nonabstract, and historical ways—not dissimilar, say, to revisionist reworkings of classical ideas and conventional wisdoms.

But deconstruction also works to dissociate itself from ideas and events that emerge out of its deconstructive labors and to prevent them from hardening into metaphysical closure, thereby keeping its messianic expectations alive and open-ended.[22] For example, while deconstruction welcomes Emmanuel Levinas's notion of responsibility to the other as a powerful critique of philosophy and ethics as conventionally understood, it also questions his arguably problematic distinction between the relation to human others and the relation to God.[23] And while deconstruction wel-

18. Caputo, *Prayers and Tears of Jacques Derrida*, 17.
19. Roberts, "Confessing Philosophy/Writing Grace," 3–4.
20. Cited in Butler, *Bodies That Matter*, 27.
21. Collins, "Thinking the Impossible."
22. Caputo, "What Do I Love When I Love My God?" 304.
23. Derrida's concern was over Levinas's conception of otherness as distinguishable, namely, we can see and know human others but not God. As Derrida asked, "When Levinas speaks of the Wholly Other [*Tout Autre*], or of the infinitely Other, does he speak of God or the other in general? . . . [Does Levinas not] set up [*s'installe*] an analogy between the relation of Moses to God and the relation of man to man, that is of every other to every other, of every other to the wholly other, to every other of the wholly other, to the utterly other of the wholly other [*de tout autre à tout autre, au tout autre de taut autre*]?" Cited in Saghafi, "'An Almost Unheard-of Analogy,'" 42–43. For Derrida, his exploration of Moses's interaction with God in Exod 33—where Moses inquires of God, "Now show

comes Michel Foucault's effort to write a history of madness *before* its capture by knowledge, it also questions his problematic assumption to be able to do that without being ensnared by knowledge.[24] "The guiding insight of deconstruction is that every structure—be it literary, psychological, social, economic, political or religious—that organizes our experience is constituted and maintained through acts of exclusion," as Mark C. Taylor has argued. "In the process of creating something, something else inevitably gets left out. These exclusive structures can become repressive—and that repression comes with consequences . . . Derrida insists that what is repressed does not disappear but always returns to unsettle every construction, no matter how secure it seems."[25]

Affirmation Not Negation

"In me and my philosophical gestures, I have always yielded to the affirmation and invisible reaffirmation of life, by passing, alas, 'through the gate of death,' my eyes fixed upon it, at every instant," as Derrida once observed.[26] The specter of death is always present in deconstruction's affirmation of life. As earlier noted, Derrida insisted that he always yielded to the affirmation and invisible reaffirmation of life, by passing "through the gate of death [with his] eyes fixed upon it, at every instant."[27] One here is reminded of the words of Jesus: "Very truly I tell you, unless a kernel of wheat falls to the ground and dies, it remains only a single seed. But if it dies, it produces many seeds. Anyone who loves their life will lose it, while anyone who hates

---

me your glory'" (v. 18), but God offers an alternative to Moses and explains, "you cannot see my face, for no one may see me and live" (v. 20)—implies that God's refusal of visibility could in fact be taken as "the *paradigm* for all relations to the other [*l'autre*],whatever it may be [*quel qu'il soit*], human or divine." Cited in Saghafi, "An Almost Unheard-of Analogy,'" 42, italics original.

24. Derrida's key criticism of Michel Foucault's *History of Madness* revolved around Foucault's claim to have presented a history of untamed madness before being caught by classical reason, whilst employing the very language and categories of reason and rationality that were used to objectify and capture madness. Derrida, "Cogito and the History of Madness," 33–34. In other words, Derrida called into question the very *raison d'être* of Foucault's project, since no "history" of a world before reason can be possible when all history itself, by definition, is about rationality and meaning in general. De Ville, "Madness and the Law," 3.

25. Taylor, "What Derrida Really Meant."

26. Derrida, "La parole," 24.

27. Derrida, "La parole," 24.

their life in this world will keep it for eternal life" (John 12:24–25). But in contrast to the Christ-follower whose faith in God leads her to expect, on the back of the gospel promise, in life after death, deconstruction holds no such expectation. As we also saw earlier, Derrida was brutally honest about his inability to accept the necessity of death, even as he claimed to believe in that "old philosophical injunction since Plato: to philosophize is to learn to die," as he put it. "I have never learned-to-live. In fact not at all!" he candidly confessed in the last interview he gave before his death. "Learning to live should mean learning to die, learning to take into account, so as to accept, absolute mortality (that is, without salvation, resurrection, or redemption—neither for oneself nor for the other)."[28] On the other hand, the biblical claim for human frailty is not rooted in an awareness let alone acceptance of mortality and death, but very much of life instead. "The affirmation of fragility and generosity comes not in the context of death, but in the glorious wonder of birth," as Walter Brueggemann observed. "There was a time when I was not, and then by the power, goodness, and mercy of God, I was and I am! I did not 'evolve,' but was loved and named by one even beyond mother and father, a self unashamed, unqualified, naked, beloved, and safe. Let not your heart be troubled!"[29]

Much as deconstruction seems to be about relentless negation, Derrida did not envisage it, however, to be an endless process because even for him—and this is a crucially important concession—*there are things that finally defy deconstruction*. Caputo calls such things "events," which for him comprise provocations and promises that call and recall, despite their perennial risk of suppression at the hands of larger and more powerful forces and ideas.[30] Despite its incessant unsettling of totalizing constructs

---

28. Derrida, *Learning to Live Finally*, 24. In a 1994 interview, Derrida offered this thought: "All my writing is on death. If I don't reach the place where I can be reconciled with death, then I will have failed. If I have one goal, it is to accept death and dying." Cited in Stephens, "Jacques Derrida."

29. Brueggemann, *Texts Under Negotiation*, 32.

30. Caputo, "Spectral Hermeneutics," 48. According to Caputo, events would include things like Johann Baptist Metz's "dangerous memories" of the irremissible past, and/or Slavoj Žižek's "fragile absolutes"—tender and vulnerable happenings at risk of being swallowed up or cancelled out by large and overarching theories and metanarratives—that persistently cry out for attention. Metz, *Faith in History and Society*, and Žižek, *Fragile Absolute*. While Caputo's conception of the event is doubtless indebted to Derrida, he also acknowledges his debt to Deleuze's notion of the event as not what occurs but as something within that which occurs, something yet to come that signals us and invites us in. Deleuze, *Logic of Sense*, 148–50.

and constructions, deconstruction is neither relativist nor nihilist. Rather, deconstruction maintains high standards of what properly constitutes the absolute and transcendental which, certainly in Derrida's case, are not easily satisfied.[31] For Derrida, there are certain things that cannot be dismantled, and he persistently insisted that deconstruction has always been affirmative and has always "delivered a yes to life."[32] Stated differently, deconstruction—or, if preferred, the notion of *différance*, which according to Derrida opens the space for the establishment of philosophy or ontotheology while also and always exceeding it[33]—is neither life nor is it the divine itself but the way to those final things; "God is not *différance*," as Caputo explained. "*Différance* is especially not a hidden God, the innermost concealed Godhead of negative theology."[34]

One here is reminded of how wisdom is presented in the book of Proverbs: "Get wisdom, get understanding; do not forget my words or turn away from them. Do not forsake wisdom, and she will protect you; love her, and she will watch over you. The beginning of wisdom is this: Get wisdom. Though it cost all you have, get understanding. Cherish her, and she will exalt you; embrace her, and she will honor you. She will give you a garland to grace your head and present you with a glorious crown" (Prov 4:5–9). Is wisdom God himself? Unlikely. Wisdom is presented as a creation/creature of God in Prov 8:22–23: "The LORD brought me forth as the first of his works, before his deeds of old; I was formed long ages ago, at the very beginning, when the world came to be." Wisdom reflects God, it is an attribute of God and is rendered available to God-seekers, but it itself is not God.[35] Could *différance*, with qualification, not be akin to wisdom, at least

---

31. Caputo, "Jacques Derrida (1930–2004)," 8.

32. Tacey, "Jacques Derrida," 5. Derrida obviously was not the first philosopher to "affirm life" despite his devastating attacks on philosophy and ontotheology. As Friedrich Nietzsche noted in his autobiographical *Ecce Homo*: "The saying of yea to life, and even to its weirdest and most difficult problems: the will to life rejoicing at its own infinite vitality in the sacrifice of its highest types—that is what I called Dionysian, that is what I meant as the bridge to the psychology of the tragic poet. Not to cast out terror and pity, or to purge one's self of dangerous passion by discharging it with vehemence,—this was Aristotle's misunderstanding of it,—but to be far beyond terror and pity and to be the eternal lust of Becoming itself—that lust which also involves the joy of destruction." Nietzsche, *Ecce Homo*, 72.

33. Derrida, "Différance," 6.

34. Caputo, *Prayers and Tears of Jacques Derrida*, 7.

35. Scripture refers to wisdom as a "her," if we go by the personification employed by Solomon in Prov 4:5–9.

the way Derrida perceived, presented, and practiced it? It bears noting that biblical wisdom as presented here is not the same as the wisdom defined by Aristotle in *Metaphysics*: "We suppose first, then, that the wise man knows all things, as far as possible"[36]—the purpose of which, per Nietzsche, is for domination and control. This is neither the intent of biblical wisdom nor that of *différance*. If the fear of God is the beginning of wisdom, and one could make the argument that Derrida intuitively understood this, then could he not have been using deconstruction, using *différance*, to try to get to God, to the messianic, via his "religion without religion"? I am not suggesting that wisdom and *différance* are one and the same; indeed, there is no reason to think the two are perfectly analogous even as we allow for some similitude between them. For that something or someone that Derrida regarded as (in his words) "undeconstructible"—that sacred reality that invites our pure and unconditional affirmation and for which (or whom) we can live without reservation—is, for Derrida, none other than the philosophical figure of the "to come" (*à venir*), the very figure of "the future" (*l'avenir*) and of hope and expectation, for which or whom he had been waiting.[37] Indeed, deconstruction is very explicit that the event for which it waits is not that which is present and already here, but that which is coming or is still to come, that which has been promised within words and things but remains hitherto unfulfilled.[38] It explains why Derrida was so thoroughly rigorous in applying deconstruction to almost everything because he was ultimately dissatisfied with nothing other than the coming of Messiah.

This is quite some distance from atheism as we formally understand it, even as Derrida insisted that he rightly passed for an atheist because the "God" he awaited was neither Yahweh, Jesus, Allah, Buddha, or some other named deity venerated in the orthodox religions. Accordingly, Derrida sought to affirm the very things he went to such lengths to deconstruct because their proclivity to totalization and metaphysical closure imprisons rather than liberates and kills rather than enlivens, despite their express aspirations toward emancipation of one form or another. A case in point is democracy, which Derrida welcomed but insisted it remains a "democracy to come" given the autoimmunity that arises from the perennial need liberal democratic systems have in balancing the twin requirements of

---

36. Aristotle, *Metaphysics*, 2.
37. Caputo, "Jacques Derrida (1930–2004)," 8.
38. Caputo, "Spectral Hermeneutics," 50.

freedom and equality.³⁹ In much the same way, justice also remains a justice to come because even though true justice cannot wait to reveal itself—the law that we have today being a poor substitute—it however is still not quite here.⁴⁰ In that respect, deconstruction is the warning label that reads "not quite and not yet" to any premature "authoritative" claim announcing the arrival of democracy or justice or God. Gayatri Spivak, who introduced the Anglophonic world to Derrida with her translation of his *Of Grammatology*, offers another definition of deconstruction: "if one wants a formula it is, among other things, a persistent critique of what one cannot not want."⁴¹ But is such a persistent critique, one that presumably cannot not be wanted, needed where the gospel is concerned? The answer for committed deconstructionists is a resounding yes because if the purpose and praxis of deconstruction is ultimately religious, then it might have everything to do with warring against the twin concerns of idolatry and injustice and paving the way to the kingdom of heaven that Christ has promised.

What Would Deconstruction Have Jesus Deconstruct?

In 2007, John D. Caputo published a remarkable book that inquired what, if Jesus were to confront the church in America in its present form, would he deconstruct?⁴² Taking a leaf from Charles Sheldon's influential *In His Steps* (1896)—from whence the acronym "WWJD" ("What Would Jesus Do?") arose and subsequently became ubiquitous (and highly lucrative to boot, as religious merchandise)—Caputo focused on Sheldon's appeal to his fellow Christians for both individual transformation and individual responsibility (Sheldon's evangelical side) and social and structural transformation (his Christian-socialist side). From there, Caputo brought those twin concerns to bear on the perceived conceits held by the American church in the early 2000s⁴³—including its capture by the Religious Right, to be sure, but

---

39. Evans, "Derrida and the Autoimmunity of Democracy," and Fritsch, "Derrida's Democracy To Come."

40. Martel, "Waiting for Justice," and Sokoloff, "Between Justice and Legality."

41. Spivak, "Bonding in Difference," 27–28.

42. Caputo, *What Would Jesus Deconstruct?*

43. Lots of similar examples could be mentioned; the one that comes most readily to my mind is William Connolly's exploration of what he called the formation of the "evangelical-capitalist resonance machine" in the United States, where he explains how it

Caputo also meant all expressions of religious extremism that lack space for independent thought and self-critique. Suggesting a possible spiritual link, no matter how tenuous and incongruous, between an American pastor in Topeka, Kansas (Sheldon) and an atheistic Parisian intellectual of Algerian-Jewish descent (Derrida), Caputo argued their shared concern over the metaphysical conceits of their respective cultural and institutional contexts led each to engage in deconstruction—not dissimilar to what, Caputo insisted, Jesus did vis-à-vis the religious hypocrisies of his day. As Caputo noted elsewhere:

> But there is no ironic distance in the religious faith of the fundamentalists. Their faith is direct, nonironic, and reactionary... They either know something that the intellectuals have forgotten; they affirm something that we must understand... At the same time, their faith is reactionary; it has been stampeded into a literalist extreme by the deracinating effects of modern technology and global capitalism. Their beliefs and practices are dangerous and uncritical and hence this allows their religion to be manipulated for nationalistic purposes, held captive by the worse forces, forces that contradict everything that Jesus and the prophets stand for.[44]

Caputo is not alone in his view of Jesus as a deconstructionist par excellence who challenged the idolatries and injustices perpetrated by the religious elite in Jerusalem. In like vein, Andrew Shepherd has argued the following:

> It is the very singularity and particularity of Jesus' ministry and the way in which his ethical behavior bends the established laws and customs, which leads to his ongoing conflict with the religious leaders of his day. Two obvious examples are the healing of the man with a shriveled hand on the Sabbath and Jesus' response to the woman caught in adultery. In each case, Jesus' understanding of the appropriate ethical response, reinterprets or bypasses the legal framework, and adheres to a higher ethical standard. Jesus "deconstructs" the law by revealing the way in which duty to the law, with its disregard for the singularity of the Other, runs the risk of "destroying, rather than saving life." Derrida's understanding that what is important is not one's adherence to law or a fulfilment of legal duties, but rather how one's ethical behavior accords

---

has made America an outlier among the older capitalist states with respect to inequality and climate denialism. Connolly, *Capitalism and Christianity, American Style*.

44. Caputo, "Power of the Powerless," 154.

with the transcendent nature of pure "justice," "hospitality" and "forgiveness," echoes Jesus' scathing rebuke of the Pharisees for the way in which their stringent adherence to the law blinded them to "the more important matters of the law—justice, mercy and faithfulness."[45]

Both Caputo's and Shepherd's claims raise an important implication highlighted by deconstruction: membership in an orthodox religion or concrete messianism alone does not guarantee that one will "see" God, let alone welcome him, if he were to show up, unannounced, at the church service or potluck. After all, the penitents in the synoptic gospels who encountered and embraced Jesus were prostitutes and publicans, not the Pharisees. Far from being "the final nail in the coffin of the old God," deconstruction is "the affirmation of the religious, not the leveling but the repetition of the religious . . ."[46] In this sense, Caputo felt it entirely accurate and appropriate to describe deconstruction as "a hermeneutics of the kingdom of God"[47]— say, how the Sermon on the Mount radically confronts and confounds worldly foundations and logics.[48] In another place, Caputo suggested that the radical revisability and renewal of things which the New Testament describes—cripples walk again, lepers are made whole, the dead rise from their graves, and human hearts are transformed—are not things that fit within metaphysical essentialism but are better captured by the terms of deconstruction.[49] Thus understood, Jesus would likely have trained his critical attention, on the one hand, on everything that pretends to be God and presumes to replace him (idolatry) and, on the other hand, on everyone who refuses their ethical responsibility toward the other (injustice); in short, our failure to love God and to love our neighbor as ourselves (Matt 22:37–39; Mark 12:30–31; Luke 10:27).

---

45. Shepherd, *Gift of the Other*, 67.

46. Caputo and Scanlon, "Introduction," 4.

47. Caputo, *What Would Jesus Deconstruct?* 29.

48. Far from a theology of power, Caputo's conception, inspired by Vattimo's "weak thought," could therefore be understood as a theology of weakness, a "theology of the event," that connects the weakness of God with the ethical imperative to serve the poor and needy. Caputo, *Weakness of God*, and Guarino, *Vattimo and Theology*.

49. Caputo, "What Do I Love When I Love My God?" 306.

Deconstruction's Promises (and Perils)
Against Idolatry

The deferral of presence turns out to imply messianic waiting and expectation, and the deconstruction of presence turns out to be not a denial of the presence of God but a critique of the idols of presence, which has at least as much to do with Moses' complaint with Aaron as with Nietzsche. It is idolatry to think that anything *present* can embody the *tout autre* or claim to be its visible form in history, the instantiation and actualization of *the* impossible, for whose coming, like teary-eyed old Augustine, deconstruction always prays and weeps.[50]

The age-old concern of theologians about the incompatibility between Athens and Jerusalem is also that of deconstruction. Going as far back to Augustine—despite his public break with Platonism, Augustine's God nonetheless remained, according to one assessment, "nine-tenths a metaphysical construction"[51]—the conflation of Yahweh of Israel with the supreme Being of Athens's philosophers produced what Heidegger called ontotheology, where the God of the Bible becomes ontologically merged with the God of metaphysics.[52] For Jan Patočka, this has certainly been the case where Christianity in Europe were concerned given its historical proclivity to ground itself "on a metaphysics of knowledge as *sophia tou kosmou*"—or knowledge of the order of the world and subordination of ethics and politics to objective knowledge—that has resulted in it having a Platonic rationalist foundation. As such, Western Christian theology itself has rested on "a 'natural' foundation, the 'supernatural' being understood as a fulfilling of the natural."[53] Deconstruction aims to pry the divine from metaphysical closure (which the work of Heidegger, for Derrida, served as both a point of entry as well as departure[54]); as Caputo and Scanlon explain, "The

---

50. Caputo and Scanlon, "Introduction," 5, italics original.

51. O'Leary, *Questioning Back*, 186.

52. Kearney, "God Who May Be," 157.

53. Patočka, *Heretical Essays in the Philosophy of History*, 119. Compelling as the reasons for ontotheology are, commentators like Martin Buber and Franz Rosenzweig remind us that what the suffering Hebrews living under conditions of slavery in Egypt and/or exile in Babylon needed most was not some metaphysical proof about the existence of Yahweh as much as the assurance that he had heard their cries and would deliver them in due course. Bowler, "Rosenzweig on Judaism and Christianity," and Buber, *Moses*.

54. As Derrida conceded, "What I have attempted to do would not have been possible without the opening of Heidegger's question . . . But despite this debt to Heidegger's thought, or rather because of it, I attempt to locate in Heidegger's text—which, no more

non-appearing of the Messiah, the non-givenness of any saturating givenness, is for Derrida a way to protect us against idols, to protect us from the Hegelian *aigle*, from divinizing something that presents itself here and now, in the present, as God's form on earth."[55] Or, as Thomas Altizer put it, "theologically, it would not be amiss to identify the deconstruction movement as a contemporary expression of demythologizing, and particularly so if we were to follow Derrida and conceive 'the logos' to be deconstructed or decentered as God's infinite understanding."[56] Thus understood, it is therefore in the context of orthodox and organized religion that deconstruction continues its relentless work of demythologization, where Derrida's personal quest for "religion without religion" necessarily persists until the real Messiah shows up, if at all. And Derrida was careful to insist that his quest was not original since similar efforts had been attempted over the years, in different respects and with different results, by thinkers as varied as Emmanuel Levinas, Jean-Luc Marion, Paul Ricoeur, Patočka, and even Kant, Hegel, Heidegger, and Kierkegaard about, in Derrida's terms, the possibility of religion without religion.[57]

We are reminded of the project of apophatic/negative theology and its claim of an absolute difference between the human and the divine such that our natural faculties are incapable of achieving comprehensive let alone complete knowledge of God (1 Cor 13:12–13). In Aquinas's words, "what the substance of God is remains in excess of our intellect and therefore is unknown to us; on account of this, *the highest human knowledge of God is to know that one does not know God*"[58]—and this coming from arguably the church's greatest scholastic who abruptly halted work on his unfinished *Summa Theologica*, silenced as it were, when Aquinas reportedly received divine revelations that rendered his writings "like straw." Hence, from Jean-Luc Marion, who prefers "mystical theology" as the label for his brand of apophasis or, perhaps more accurately, a cataphatic conception of divinity so rich and saturated it precludes apprehension: "Even if we were to comprehend God as such (by naming him in terms of his presence), we would

---

than any other, is not homogeneous, continuous, everywhere equal to the greatest force and to all the consequences of its questions—the signs of a belonging to metaphysics, or to what he calls ontotheology." Derrida, *Positions*, 4.

55. Caputo and Scanlon, "Introduction," 8.
56. Cited in Taylor, "Altizer's Derrida," 49.
57. Derrida, *Gift of Death*, 49.
58. Cited in Marion, "In His Name," 35, italics mine.

at once be knowing not God as such, but less than God, because we could easily conceive of another still greater than the one we comprehend. For the one we comprehend would always remain less than and below the one we do not comprehend."[59] Or as Regina Mara Schwartz has argued, "Neither a realistic nor a utopian *description* can capture divinity, because no description, not even beautiful ones, capture the divine."[60] No word or concept or signification, always and already limited and imperfect, can hope to capture the divine; far from putting us in the presence of God, that word or concept only ends up cutting God down to size.[61] Furthermore, while the aims of such efforts by theological thinkers have in mind the restoration of the integrity of the Christian faith, other efforts by nonreligious or even antireligious thinkers—Marx, Nietzsche, Freud, and so forth—helped nudge the apophatic enterprise toward a radical "death of God" orientation, which proffered "a world in which God, through the act of kenosis, has fully emptied Godself . . . [and where] the idea of God is no more than a human projection."[62] For Marion—with whom Derrida shared much but also had key differences—the broader effort to maintain silence about God by way of apophasis runs the risk of silencing and domesticating God, if inadvertently, where we protect ourselves against "being seized by what we do not see."[63] For that reason, Marion argues, contra deconstruction, that to utter God's name is never to fix his essence in terms of presence because God's presence always and already exceeds his essence[64]—or "God without Being," as Marion has stated elsewhere.[65] Furthermore, pushing the apo-

59. Marion, "In His Name," 36.

60. Schwartz, "Questioning Narratives of God," 215, italics original.

61. The Bible writers' gratuitous reliance on symbolic language to describe God—awesome but ultimately vain attempts at that—underscores both Schwartz's and Marion's points. Take, for example, Ezekiel's vision of God: "Above the vault over their heads was what looked like a throne of lapis lazuli, and high above on the throne was a figure like that of a man. I saw that from what appeared to be his waist up he looked like glowing metal, as if full of fire, and that from there down he looked like fire; and brilliant light surrounded him. Like the appearance of a rainbow in the clouds on a rainy day, so was the radiance around him. This was the appearance of the likeness of the glory of the Lord" (Ezek 1:26–28a). No available words and phrases—e.g., "what looked," "like that of a," "what appeared to be," "the appearance of the likeness of"—could adequately capture the divine.

62. Robbins, "Introduction," 9.

63. Westphal, "Overcoming Onto-theology," 161.

64. Marion, "In His Name," 29.

65. Marion, *God Without Being*.

phatic argument to its extreme raises the interrelated problem of distancing God from us to the point of writing off his activity on earth. As Richard Kearney has argued against negative theology's aim to put God beyond the proper names of Being: "If God is devoid of historical being, is He not then also deprived of the power to act and call and love—a God so distant as to be defunct?"[66]

But here lies a key difference: Although they share the view of God or the messianic as wholly other, deconstruction is not the same as apophatic/negative theology or Marion's mystical theology, however, because the latter two conceptions are always and already hyper-essentialist, that is, they seek a higher affirmation of a God or Godhead beyond "God." (Recall Meister Eckhart's plea, "I pray God to rid me of God," in order that he might rise above man's flawed interpretations of God and see God as he truly is.) Far as Derrida were concerned, apophatic/negative and mystical theologies' refusal to let go of an absolute point of view—what he called *hyperousiology*[67]—is where he drew the line between them and deconstruction because they are always going about the Father's business, they aim ultimately to save the eminence of the Christian God.[68] In the final analysis, negative and mystical theologians continue to uphold an "idol of some naked prelinguistic ineffable given" despite their critique of idolatry.[69] In

---

66. Kearney, "God Who May Be," 158.

67. Caputo, *Prayers and Tears of Jacques Derrida*, 34.

68. Caputo, "Apostles of the Impossible," 188. To be sure, Marion might have insisted his goal is not to be hyper-essentialist and that he is against a metaphysics of presence, but as both Derrida and Caputo argue, his mystical theology fails to escape a mystical economy—as in Marion's notion of *denominating* God or uttering the name of God in praise of him—which the latter insist is but another form of hyper-essentialism. Caputo, "Apostles of the Impossible," 189–90, and Marion, "In His Name."

69. Caputo, "Power of the Powerless," 117. One may recall Derrida's reflections on Nietzsche. Against the erroneous charge that Nietzsche's work is nihilistic and relativistic—indeed, those were the qualities he saw as characteristic of modern civilization which he fought hard against because, far as he was concerned, they misrepresented "the world of existence" as he experienced and understood it through his naturalist lens—there does appear to be a kind of tacit "Archimedean point"—despite his ferocious attack metaphysics and the Cartesian cogito—from which Nietzsche historized, critiqued, and condemned Christian morality. Nietzsche, *Will to Power*, 23, and Monte, "Sum, Ergo Cogito." Referring to Nietzsche's genealogy of morality as the effort to "get behind" the moral and the political, Derrida for example argued that Nietzsche's work is in a sense metaethical because it reaffirms—or, at the very least, it presumes—the possibility of what Derrida called the "arche-ethical or ultra-ethical"—a law behind the law, so to speak. Derrida and Beardsworth, "Nietzsche and the Machine." Moreover, Nietzsche's move is no less metaphysical since all that he so ably deciphered obviously had to be, by

short, the very act of protesting against ontotheology ends up unwittingly as an ontotheological gesture.[70] For the same reason, Derrida took pains to distinguish deconstruction from Heidegger's notion of destruction or negation of metaphysics because he saw Heidegger's attempt to reverse metaphysics and ontotheology as intrinsically bound to the ontological structure and vocabulary of metaphysics, never quite able to escape it even though Heidegger sought to "destroy" it.[71] Furthermore, and in the same vein, in riposte to the claim that the Bible constitutes the inspired, infallible, and inerrant word of God, deconstruction would likely insist that Holy Writ is but an archive rather than the arche, a chronicle rather than the cause, and the proclivity among fundamentalists and scriptural literalists to conflate the two is to succumb to the idolatry of a book through making an idol out of an icon.[72] Indeed, Caputo would urge Christians to go beyond the unreflective reception and acceptance of church teaching and tradition and to move toward a "deeper affirmation" of the love of Christ. Contending that release from idolatry is the part of the relief, the good news, that postmodernism and specifically deconstruction offers to the church, Caputo writes:

> The Scriptures, in turn, do not relieve us of the responsibility of thinking for ourselves (*supere aude*) or of rethinking ancient traditions, for the ultimate tradition that is handed down to us is not any particular creed, practice, or institutional structure, but the event of love that was astir in Jesus and then is handed on to the church. Derrida would say that a genuine tradition is not constituted by any position or positivity but by a deeper affirmation.[73]

It is hard to disagree with Caputo's good news about the benefits deconstruction has to offer the gospel. That said, in view of deconstruction's relentless critique against idolatry and its suspicions over the ironical outcomes of presumptuous efforts to destroy metaphysics, it is perhaps understandable why Derrida arguably resisted the hypostatic claim concerning the incarnate Christ—why Derrida apparently refused the possibility that Jesus could be the Messiah for whom he had all along been waiting—because that, fairly or otherwise, could be to confuse icon (i.e.,

---

his own reasoning, decipherable to begin with. Spivak, "Translator's Preface," xxiv.
70. Westphal, "Overcoming Onto-theology," 161.
71. Botha, "From Destruktion to Deconstruction."
72. Caputo, *What Would Jesus Deconstruct?* 104.
73. Caputo, *What Would Jesus Deconstruct?* 112.

Jesus as the full representation of God) with idol.⁷⁴ It is worth bearing in mind that the notion that the Son of God as both fully divine and fully human, a cardinal emphasis in mainstream Christology and what Kierkegaard referred to as the absolute paradox in his *Philosophical Fragments*, was and remains controversial in some circles; as Maimonides (otherwise known as Moses ben Maimon, the influential Torah scholar of the Middle Ages) observed, the most serious theological error consists in the imputation of corporeality to God, one that invites idolatry through the notion that a particular form represents the agent between God and his creation.⁷⁵ "Something has not yet arrived, neither at Christianity nor by means of Christianity," as Derrida once mused. "What has not yet arrived at or happened to Christianity is Christianity. Christianity has not yet come to

---

74. While Derrida did not discuss the work of Paul Tillich, his logic here resonates somewhat with Tillich's claim that there is a God hidden behind the back of Jesus Christ. By positing the doctrine of God's hiddenness which stands over and against Jesus Christ, Tillich went as far as to insist that "Jesus of Nazareth is sacrificed to Jesus as the Christ," implying therefore that God is mostly unknown (by revelation), that there is in fact a deep abyss hidden behind God's self-revelation in Jesus Christ, and that one therefore ought to seriously consider the meaning of the Christian message *apart from Jesus*. Tillich, *Systematic Theology*, 135. Which essentially amounted to the claim that Jesus of Nazareth is an unreliable source of knowledge for Jesus the Christ, and thus the need to assume and assert a God that is hidden behind Jesus Christ. McKelway, *Systematic Theology of Paul Tillich*, 5–7. While Karl Barth's caveat that one should avoid any immature or superficial critique of Tillich is well taken, the possibility that Tillich's work fails, deliberately or otherwise, to proclaim the revelation of God in Jesus Christ cannot be dismissed.

75. Maimonides, *Guide for the Perplexed*, 51–52. Or take, for example, Edith Wyschogrod's suggestion that the Decalogue (Ten Commandments) that God supplied his people could be considered a simulacrum that invites interpretation. The "original" set of tablets that were inscribed by the finger of God (Exod 31:18) were destroyed by Moses in his anger when confronting the Israelites over their idolatry with the golden calf (Exod 32:19). But although God promised to rewrite the Decalogue to replace the broken first set (Exod 34:1, 4), it turned out that the second set of tablets were in fact chiseled and copied by Moses, however (Exod 34:27–28). Wyschogrod, "Eating the Text, Defiling the Hands," 253. For Wyschogrod, the second set of tablets, for all intents and purposes a simulacrum whose contents are now open to interpretation and even idolization because the Word of God had been mediated through man (Moses), exemplified Derrida's reflections on the question of repetition in *Specters of Marx*: "Repetition *and* first time: this is perhaps the question of the event as question of the ghost. What is a ghost? What is the *effectivity* of the presence of a specter that is of what seems to remain as ineffective, virtual, insubstantial as a simulacrum? Is there *there*, between the thing itself and its simulacrum, an opposition that holds up? Repetition *and* first time, but also repetition and last time, since the singularity of any first time makes of it also a last time." Derrida, *Specters of Marx*, 10, italics original.

Christianity."[76] Yet believing that Christ already came in the flesh does not, I suggest, invalidate Derrida's insistence that Christianity has not yet come to Christianity, since Christians await Christ's second coming (a key point that awaits fuller treatment in the fourth chapter). For Christ-followers, Christ and his kingdom have come (Luke 17:20–21), but they still await its fulfillment in all its fullness and wholeness, and hence Christians continue to say, "Maranatha!" Nowhere is this notion of "already but not yet" more evident than in the Lord's Prayer, where the nexus between the present and the future is underscored whenever believers participate in that prayer, where "the time and place where God the King is honored, where his reign is clear and absolute, and therefore, his sovereign will happens."[77] That said, it is one thing for deconstruction to say that Jesus would have deconstructed our idolatrous efforts to domesticate him for our comfort—a *Baalism redivivus*, as Eugene Peterson put it.[78] It is quite another for deconstruction to exercise a form of positivism in historicizing him—per deconstruction's expectations, Jesus could not be Messiah since he already "came," in the flesh no less, and therefore could not be the Messiah still to come—or even vilify him and vindicate its rejection (in Derrida's case, an indefinite suspension of judgment) of Jesus's purported divinity.[79] The crucial implications of deconstruction's stance here for Christology will be taken up in the next chapter.

Against Injustice

> It is *always* in the name of ethics—a supposedly democratic ethics of discussion—it is always in the name of transparent communication and "consensus" that the most brutal disregard of the elementary rules of discussion is produced (by these elementary rules, I mean differentiated reading or listening to the other, proof, argumentation, analysis, and quotation). It is *always* the moralistic discourse of consensus—at least the discourse that pretends to

---

76. Jacques Derrida, *Points*, 28.
77. Pennington, *Sermon on the Mount*, 224.
78. Peterson, *Five Smooth Stones for Pastoral Work*, 84.
79. Lest we judge Derrida and deconstruction too harshly on this point, let us bear in mind that some of the greatest theological minds in Protestant Christianity—think of Rudolf Bultmann, Karl Barth, or even Dietrich Bonhoeffer—were also of the view that the eschaton had already been realized. Burley, "Dislocating the Eschaton?" and Congdon, "Bonhoeffer and Bultmann."

appeal sincerely to consensus—that produces in fact the indecent transgression of the classical norms of reason and democracy.[80]

The second broad concern has to do with injustice. Derrida identified justice as outside of or beyond manmade law, and forgiveness and hospitality as equally outside of or beyond manmade ethics, regarding such as transcendentals that presumably harbor no "always-already hidden contradictions" and therefore defy deconstruction.[81] Here too his quest for justice, forgiveness, and hospitality is no less the quest for Messiah. Indebted to Levinas's notion of ethics as the ceaseless and holistic responsibility that one bears to the other(s),[82] including God—although Derrida had his issues with Levinas's conception, which he judged as still too metaphysical[83]—Derrida envisaged a relationship with the other that transgresses the economy of calculation, limitation, and reciprocity. As Derrida once noted about gifts, our conventional conception of a gift tends to be confined within the economy of calculation and reciprocity—think, for instance, of the practice of gift exchanges at Christmas—but what makes something truly a gift is its tendency toward excessiveness that "overrun[s] the border."[84] As Derrida once argued about what makes justice truly just:

> Justice, if it has to do with the other, with the infinite distance of the other, is always unequal to the other, is always incalculable. You cannot calculate justice. Levinas says somewhere that the definition of justice—which is very minimal but which I love, which I think is really rigorous—is that justice is the relation to the other. That is all. Once you relate to the other as the other, then something incalculable comes on the scene, something which cannot be reduced to the law or to the history of legal structures.[85]

And if such an uncompromising definition of justice is what deconstruction offers, then its indictment against professed Christ-followers for

---

80. Derrida, *Memoires*, 400.

81. Derrida, "Force of Law," and Derrida, "Hostipitality."

82. As Derrida wrote, "Hospitality is culture itself and not simply one ethic among others. Insofar as it had to do with the *ethos*, that is, the residence, one's home, the familiar place of dwelling, inasmuch as it is a manner of being there, the manner in which we relate to ourselves and to others, to others as our own or foreigners, *ethics is hospitality*; ethics is so thoroughly coextensive with the experience of hospitality." Derrida, *On Cosmopolitanism and Forgiveness*, 3, italics original.

83. Derrida, "Violence and Metaphysics."

84. Derrida, *Given Time*, 91.

85. Derrida, *Deconstruction in a Nutshell*, 17–18.

failing to love their neighbor—the man on skid row, the woman who aborts an unwanted pregnancy, the illegal immigrant from south of the border, the fellow American who votes differently or holds a different stance on anti-coronavirus vaccinations and the wearing of facial prophylactics than they—is likely indefensible far as a Christian rejoinder were concerned. "If we ask, 'What would Jesus deconstruct?' about many Christian churches, my own guess is that he would not know where to start—with their militarism and imperialism or with their greed and indifference to the poor," as Caputo has acutely observed. "The closest thing they represent to anything Jesus encountered in his own lifetime was called 'Rome.' He simply would not recognize himself."[86]

Furthermore, Derrida questioned whether Christianity has sufficiently thematized what responsibility ought to be. His insistence on the purported unknowability (and unnameability) of God will be addressed in the next chapter but for now, it is enough to note that for Derrida, a God who cannot be, who does not allow himself to be seen, is not a sufficient condition for a principle of Christian responsibility to be established. The Christian God is not the Platonic Good: "A personal gaze, that is, a face, a figure, and not a sun. The Good becomes personal Goodness, a gaze that sees me without my seeing it."[87] The human relates not to an objectively knowable transcendent object such as the Platonic Good but to Yahweh, who not only transfixes the human by his gaze without himself being visible or accessible[88]—as the apostle John reminds us, no one has ever seen God (John 1:18)—but whose demand for Christian responsibility is uncompromising as it is unconditional. Nowhere is this more clearly expressed than in the Sermon on the Mount, where Jesus's audience is enjoined to engage in the spiritual disciplines and to do good works—prayer to God, fasting, giving to the needy—in secret because their heavenly Father, *who is unseen and who sees what is done in secret*, would reward them (Matt 6:4, 6, 18). In Derrida's perspective, the relationship is grossly unequal not only because of the vast power differential between God and human, but because the human has no way to relate to an invisible and inaccessible God, the *tout autre*, other than out of pure obligation. Accordingly, the Christian "recognizes neither debt nor duty to his fellows because he is in a relationship to God—*a relationship*

---

86. Caputo, *What Would Jesus Deconstruct?* 103.

87. Derrida, *Gift of Death*, 93.

88. Gasché, "European Memories," and Goldman, "Christian Mystery and Responsibility Gnosticism in Derrida's *The Gift of Death*."

without relation because God is absolutely transcendent, hidden, and secret, not giving any reason he can share in exchange for this doubly given death, not sharing anything in this dissymmetrical alliance."[89] Nowhere is the absolute dissymmetry of this relationship and the inconclusiveness it brings more evident for Derrida than in Paul's injunction to work out our salvation "in fear and trembling." Derrida's following reflections from his book *The Gift of Death* are worth rehearsing in some detail:

> In the Epistle to the Phil 2:12, the disciples are asked to work towards their salvation in fear and trembling. They will have to work for their salvation knowing all along that it is God who decides: the Other has no reason to give to us and nothing to settle in our favor, no reason to share his reasons with us. We fear and tremble because we are already in the hands of God, although free to work, but in the hands and under the gaze of God, whom we don't see and whose will we cannot know, no more than the decisions he will hand down, nor his reasons for wanting this or that, our life or death, our salvation or perdition. We fear and tremble before the inaccessible secret of a God who decides for us although we remain responsible, that is, free to decide, to work, to assume our life and our death.[90]

For Derrida, the absolute demands of this terribly absolutist God are such that they impel the Christian toward unethical and irresponsible conduct toward even her family and friends. Following Kierkegaard in *Fear and Trembling*,[91] Derrida saw God's impossible demand on Abraham to sacrifice his son Isaac atop Mount Moriah as *a transgression of responsibility to the other*—not only toward Isaac but also other members of Abraham's family to and for whom he was responsible:

> ... Kierkegaard reflects on this double secret: that between God and Abraham but also that between the latter and his family. Abraham doesn't speak of what God has ordered him alone to do, he doesn't speak of it to Sarah, or to Eliezer, or to Isaac. He must keep the secret (that is his duty), but it is also a secret that he *must* keep as a double necessity because in the end he *can only* keep it: he doesn't know it, he is unaware of its ultimate rhyme and reason. He is sworn to secrecy because he is in secret. Because, in this way, he doesn't speak, Abraham transgresses the ethical order. According

---

89. Derrida, *Gift of Death*, 72–73, italics mine.
90. Derrida, *Gift of Death*, 56.
91. Kierkegaard, *Fear and Trembling*.

to Kierkegaard, the highest expression of the ethical is in terms of what binds us to our own and to our fellows (that can be the family but also the actual community of friends or the nation). By keeping the secret, Abraham betrays ethics.[92]

Thus understood, obedience to the biblical God could well lead to the irresponsible and unjust treatment of others. As Jesus insisted on the cost of discipleship, "If anyone comes to me and does not hate father and mother, wife and children, brothers and sisters—yes, even their own life—such a person cannot be my disciple" (Luke 14:26).[93] The secrecy in which Abraham was forced to participate, which led him to betray ethics through the sacrifice of Isaac and the forced silence over his planned filicide with his wife and servants, is in the end intolerable for ethics, philosophy, and politics for which there can be no "final secrets."[94] Derrida referred to this as the aporia of responsibility:

> Here on the contrary it appears, just as necessarily, that the absolute responsibility of my actions, to the extent that such a responsibility remains mine, singularly so, something no one else can perform in my place, instead implies secrecy. But what is also implied is that, by not speaking to others, I don't account for my actions, that I answer for nothing [*que je ne reponde de rien*] and to no one, that I make no response to others or before others. It is both a scandal and a paradox. According to Kierkegaard, *ethical* exigency is regulated by and it therefore defines a responsibility that consists of *speaking*, that is, of involving oneself sufficiently in the generality to justify oneself, to give an account of one's decision and to answer for one's actions. On the other hand, what does Abraham teach us, in his approach to sacrifice? That far from ensuring responsibility, the generality of ethics incites to irresponsibility. It impels me to speak, to reply, to account for something, and thus to dissolve my singularity in the medium of the concept. Such is the aporia of responsibility: one always risks not managing

---

92. Derrida, *Gift of Death*, 59, italics original.

93. In Derrida's terms: "If I put to death or grant death to what I hate it is not a sacrifice. I must sacrifice what I love. I must come to hate what I love, in the same moment, at the instant of granting death. I must hate and betray my own, that is to say offer them the gift of death by means of the sacrifice, not insofar as I hate them, that would be too easy, but insofar as I love them. I must hate them insofar as I love them. Hate wouldn't be hate if it only hated the hateful, that would be too easy. It must hate and betray what is most lovable. Hate cannot be hate, it can only be the sacrifice of love to love." Derrida, *Gift of Death*, 64.

94. Derrida, *Gift of Death*, 63.

to accede to the concept of responsibility in the process of *forming* it . . . The ethical can therefore end up making us irresponsible.[95]

The impossible and, from an ethical standpoint, irresponsible demands of the God of the Bible—"the unique, jealous, secret God," the one to whom we, like Abraham, say "Here I am," and who impels his followers to betray ethics[96]—do not, in Derrida's view, allow for an adequate thematization of Christian responsibility. And yet could it not be argued, contra Derrida but in line with the logic of deconstruction, that the betrayal of ethics (as he understood it) for the sake of a higher ethical calling vis-à-vis the divine Other, is in fact the most deconstructive of moves? Consider, for example: the two Hebrew midwives who dared disobey Pharoah's kill order against Hebrew baby boys because the midwives feared God more than they did the king of Egypt (Exod 1:15–17); the prostitute Rahab who engaged in treason to save two Hebrew spies (Josh 2:1–6); Obadiah, administrator in King Ahab's palace, who, at risk of his own well-being, hid a hundred of Yahweh's prophets in two caves from his queen Jezebel's murderous wrath (1 Kgs 18:4), and so on. We may recall Baudelaire's observation that whenever he encountered virtuous conduct by others, they always proved to be encounters against the nature of things[97]; perhaps this may include running against the grain of the prevailing ethical norms of one's place and time.[98]

Crucially, Derrida's account of Abraham fails to account for that fact that Abraham had a relationship with God that presumably began with God's call to Abraham issued as far back as Gen 12:1–3. As observed a few pages earlier regarding possible objections against the insistence, shared by apophatic/negative theology and deconstruction, on God as the absolute and wholly other of which we can know nothing, what the Genesis narrative indicates otherwise is that God and Abraham had a history together; in short, Abraham knew enough about the Other which enabled him, doubtless in fear and trembling nonetheless (Phil 2:12), to step forth in

---

95. Derrida, *Gift of Death*, 60–61, italics original.
96. Derrida, *Gift of Death*, 62.
97. Sturm, "Charles Baudelaire," 28.
98. An example might be Nietzsche's *On the Genealogy of Morality*, which he wrote partly as a counter to the perceived destructiveness of nihilism and "the uselessness" of pessimism that, far as he was concerned, was perpetrated by the extant Judeo-Christian system of moral values and virtues. And yet Nietzsche's goal was not the rejection of ethics and morals but the pursuit of such in his own fashion. Stern, *Nietzsche's Ethics*.

obedience into the unknown. Indeed, Abraham was sufficiently emboldened to approach God, "negotiate" with him, and extract from him certain assurances surrounding his planned destruction of Sodom (Gen 18:20–33). That Abraham even dared to do so implies a relationship he had with God that was predicated upon intimate knowledge of the other—incomplete, to be sure, but no less intimate for the man referred to as "God's friend" (Jas 2:23)—concerning the latter's reliability and trustworthiness. Abraham, in Kierkegaard's words, "believed, and believed for this life."[99] As Kierkegaard averred:

> Yea, if [Abraham's] faith had been only for a future life, he surely would have cast everything away in order to hasten out of this world to which he did not belong. But Abraham's faith was not of this sort, if there be such a faith; for really this is not faith but the furthest possibility of faith which has a presentiment of its object at the extremest limit of the horizon, yet is separated from it by a yawning abyss within which despair carries on its game. But Abraham believed precisely for this life, that he was to grow old in the land, honored by the people, blessed in his generation, remembered forever in Isaac, his dearest thing in life, whom he embraced with a love for which it would be a poor expression to say that he loyally fulfilled the father's duty of loving the son, as indeed is evinced in the words of the summons, "the son whom thou lovest." Jacob had twelve sons, and one of them he loved; Abraham had only one, the son whom he loved.[100]

And as discussed, Derrida's likely resistance to the incarnate Christ as Messiah, to Jesus as the full representation of God, meant he would not have entertained much less accepted the second part of John 1:18, "the one and only Son, who is himself God and is in closest relationship with the Father, *has made him known*." That God is knowable and indeed has been made known through his Son—as Jesus said, "Anyone who has seen me has seen the Father" (John 14:9b)[101]—seems beyond the horizon of acceptability for deconstruction. For Patočka, God's apparent invisibility and

---

99. "I remain confident of this: I will see the goodness of the Lord in the land of the living," as King David put it. "Wait for the Lord; be strong and take heart and wait for the Lord" (Ps 27:13–14).

100. Kierkegaard, *Fear and Trembling*, 17.

101. In that same dialogue with his disciples, Jesus also said, "If you really know me, you will know my Father as well. From now on, you do know him and have seen him" (John 14:7).

inaccessibility connoted an inadequate thematic development within the perspective of Christianity[102]; for Derrida, as we have seen, divine invisibility and inaccessibility connoted the purported inability of Christianity to thematize response and responsibility, that is, what a responsible person is or ought to be.[103] As he argued elsewhere concerning religion as being all about humankind's response—and, by extension, responsibility—to the divine, to the wholly other, the *tout autre*: "Response: Religion is the *Response*. Is it not there, perhaps, that we must seek the beginning of a response? Assuming, that is, that one knows what responding means, and also responsibility. Assuming, that is, that one knows it—and believes in it. No response, indeed, without a principle of responsibility. One must respond to the other, before the other, and for oneself."[104] Accordingly, an invisible and unknowable God whose demand for absolute obedience causes his followers to behave irresponsibly and unjustly toward others renders difficult the development of a principle of human responsibility. Any meaningful redress of this problem would necessarily require a decisive break from Christianity's residual and unacknowledged debt to the Platonic model—Christianity's "incorrigible Platonism," as Derrida put it.[105] But an answer to that, in good deconstructive fashion, will have to be deferred for now.

Hallelujah to a Godless God?

Deconstruction promises much that is crucially beneficial to a Christianity replete with idols of its own making and injustices of its own doing. But deconstruction is clearly not without its perils. Commendable as its unequivocal commitment to the smashing of idols and its urgent call for justice are, its steadfast aspiration to transcend all concrete messianisms—to go beyond "a proper or identifiable Giver which gives us a proper or identifiable Gift"[106]—implies a desire for a "Godless God,"[107] a messiah that

102. Patočka, *Heretical Essays in the Philosophy of History*, 116.
103. Derrida, *Gift of Death*, 25.
104. Derrida, "Faith and Knowledge," 26.
105. Derrida, *Gift of Death*, 28. Others have taken umbrage with what they see as Derrida's idiosyncratic, even inaccurate, reading of Patočka's account of Christianity. Findlay, *Caring for the Soul in a Postmodern Age*.
106. Caputo, *Prayers and Tears of Jacques Derrida*, 165.
107. Kearney, "Desire of God," 124.

ironically, for all deconstruction's relentless work in demythologization, awaits fabrication. As Caputo and Michael Scanlon have explained:

> Derrida . . . does not dismiss God per se, but he insists on a general openness to an alterity without name, without identity, which he calls the 'Messianic' in contradistinction to any particular 'messianism' of positive revelation . . . So Derrida's desire of God is an impossible God of such indeterminate and undefined alterity that *it will always remain to be invented.*[108]

But until that messiah is finally revealed or invented—indeed, even after all that—the hallelujah that deconstruction offers its no-show Godless God, to borrow from one of Leonard Cohen's songs, can only be a cold and very broken one, fraught, it seems, with endless prayers and tears tied to an impossibly heavy burden of its own making.

---

108. Caputo and Scanlon, "Introduction," 13, italics mine.

3

Awaiting Deconstruction's Impossible God

To an unknown God (Acts 17:23).

God neither could have been, nor ought to have been, unknown. Could not have been, because of His greatness; ought not to have been, because of His goodness . . .[1]

THAT DECONSTRUCTION HAS MUCH to offer the gospel is evident. Its aim, so claimed, is to affirm—to always deliver "a yes to life"—rather than to negate. The Christ-follower is called to love God with heart, soul, mind, and strength, and to love her neighbor as herself—divine commands which continue to be resisted because of humankind's proclivity toward idolatry and injustice. Glimpses of possibilities exist—think, for example, of the ledger of "positives" alongside "negatives" enumerated by "the First and the Last," the "Living One" who holds the keys of death and Hades, in his message to the seven churches in Asia Minor in Rev 2 and 3—but the heavenly kingdom of God envisioned by Jesus in his Sermon on the Mount remains largely a vision yet to be fulfilled by an earthbound Church persistently mired in all forms of idolatry and injustice. As John Caputo has powerfully argued in his book *What Would Jesus Deconstruct?* there is much that deconstruction, whose very purpose and praxis are ostensibly religious in nature, can contribute to nudging the earthly Church in its transformative journey toward becoming the kingdom of heaven. Ingeniously positioning

---

1. Tertullian, *Writings of Tertullian—Volume II*, 65.

Jesus as a deconstructionist par excellence, Caputo insists that deconstruction is in effect "a hermeneutics of the kingdom of God."[2]

On the other hand, Caputo's argument stands in contrast to Derrida's longstanding resistance to what he called "concrete messianisms," that is, the world's orthodox faiths and their respective messiahs—Yahweh, Jesus, Allah, Buddha, and so forth, but equally other wholly others such as democracy, justice, and truth. For my purposes, nowhere is this more evident than Derrida's apparent rejection—or, more charitably, his indefinite suspension of judgment—of the incarnate Christ as Messiah, as we shall see below. The reasons for his resistance partly had to do with the history of violence and injustice with which he associated the determinate religions; as Caputo has written elsewhere, "Derrida's distinction between the concrete messianisms and the messianic in general is, we cannot forget, a distinction between war and peace."[3] If Islam has given the world "bloody borders"—so claimed the famed political scientist Samuel Huntington in his provocative 1993 essay, "The Clash of Civilizations"[4]—then that, far as Derrida was concerned, is true not only of Islam but of Christianity as well. For Derrida, the Messiah, if he/she/it exists at all—that sacred reality that delivers peace rather than war and that invites our pure and unconditional affirmation and for which (or whom) we can live without reservation—remains an eschatological hope always still "to come" (*à venir*).[5] As such, all existing claims that Messiah has already come—or, at the very least, has been identified or is identifiable—are to be treated with suspicion as idols rendered by human hands and metaphysical cum ontotheological conceits that deserve to be critiqued and dismantled. Hence Derrida's rigorous and relentless application of deconstruction to almost everything in sight because he ultimately was dissatisfied with nothing other than the coming of Messiah.

What, then, are we to make of the distinction between a deconstruction that the gospel cannot do without, on the one hand, and deconstruction's seeming refusal to acknowledge the biblical Jesus as the Messiah for which it awaits on the other? We may recall, for instance, how Augustine—despite his indebtedness to Platonism for leading him beyond materialism and toward the Christian gospel[6]—saw the efforts of the Platonists

---

2. Caputo, *What Would Jesus Deconstruct?* 29.
3. Caputo, *Prayers and Tears of Jacques Derrida*, 195.
4. Huntington, "Clash of Civilizations?"
5. Caputo, "Jacques Derrida (1930–2004)," 8.
6. Biemiller, "Augustine and Plato," 33–34, and Kenney, "'None Come Closer to Us

as equally a bridge to the gospel, but one which they themselves failed to cross because they did not acknowledge the fundamentals of the gospel like the incarnation and resurrection of Christ.[7] Deconstruction can furnish a remarkable service in the philosophical and theological spaces through, to paraphrase the apostle Paul, demolishing arguments and pretensions that set themselves up against the knowledge of God—but, crucially in Derrida's case, *without* taking captive thoughts and subjecting them in obedience to Christ (2 Cor 10:5). Indeed, it is not impossible that Derrida, so given to the notions of impossibility and the impossible God,[8] might have ironically slammed shut the door to the prospect of the biblical Jesus as the coming Messiah.

Aporia and Undecidability

In Samuel Beckett's play *Waiting for Godot*, the main protagonists Vladimir and Estragon meet on a country road by a leafless tree and engage in a variety of discussions and encounters while awaiting the titular Godot, who never arrives. At one point, Estragon exclaims, "Nothing happens, nobody comes, nobody goes, it's awful!" (Contrary to popular opinion, *Seinfeld* was not the first theatrical production about nothing!) Likewise, deconstruction is engaged in an indefinite wait for Messiah to show up, a deferral that is itself endless. The incessant deferral at the heart of Derrida's conception of *différance* (introduced briefly in the previous chapter), which denotes not only difference but crucially the deferral of meaning, places him indefinitely within an aporetic moment from which he is either unable or unwilling to depart. There are numerous examples—Derrida wrote endlessly about it—of deconstruction's emphasis on aporia and undecidability, but the following illustration would do quite nicely. Taking aim at Francis Fukuyama's controversial claim, made in the closing stages of the Cold War, that history ended with the collapse of communism that left democracy

---

than These.'"

7. Chang, *Engaging Unbelief*, 8. As Augustine concluded, "Likewise, the praise with which I so greatly extolled Plato and the Platonists (or the Academic philosophers) was most inappropriate for these impious persons and has rightly displeased me; it is especially in the face of their great errors that Christian teaching must be defended." Augustine, *Revisions (Retractationes)*, 29. This obviously has been complicated by Augustine's reported inability, as well as that of the other patristic authors, to escape fully from metaphysics and ontotheology. O'Leary, *Questioning Back*.

8. Rayment-Pickard, *Impossible God*.

and capitalism as the undisputed winners of the ideological war,[9] Derrida decried Fukuyama's bold contention as "gospel," "neo-testamentary," "neo-evangelistic," and "essentially a Christian eschatology"—an attempt to construct and justify a modern-day version of the city of God.[10] But the litany of conflicts and wars that have taken place since the fall of communism—the Gulf War, 9/11, Afghanistan, Iraq, Ukraine, and everything else in between—exposed the end-of-history claim as yet another false dawn—and another false Christ, Derrida would likely have insisted—promised and proclaimed by false prophets.[11] For all intents and purposes, democracy, like the messianic, remains something still "to come" (*la démocratie à venir*). Indeed, Derrida insisted that deconstruction lacks the authority to resolve aporia and undecidability.[12]

This is not to imply that deconstruction's apparent rejection of the biblical Jesus—or some other preferred divine personage or entity—as Messiah is thereby final and absolute. Nowhere is this heightened sensitivity to aporia and undecidability more evident than in Derrida's hesitancy over the question of whether messianism is a universal and abstract phenomenon or something particular to a determinate religion or indeed singularly irreducible events such as the nativity and the passion of Christ. (I will return to the third of these possibilities later.) As Jeffrey Hanson has noted,

> Derrida was never able to settle fully the question of whether the structure of religion without religion, messianicity without messianism, was itself universal or quasi-universal, abstract, and thus independent of the positive traditions of the religions of the Book

---

9. Fukuyama, *End of History and the Last Man*.

10. Derrida, *Specters of Marx*, 75–76.

11. Musing on the readiness of some to adopt an apocalyptic orientation—say, in summarily declaring the end of philosophy, or the end of history as in Fukuyama's case, or the end of theology—Derrida once recalled Kant's impatience against this trend in "mystagogy" or the practice of mysticism: "These people place themselves out of the common, but they have this in common: they are all in immediate and intuitive relation with the mystery . . . The mystagogues claim to possess as it were in private the privilege of a mysterious secret . . . The revelation or unveiling of the secret is reserved to them . . . each newcomer, more lucid than the other, more vigilant and more prodigal too than the other, coming to add more to it: . . . the end of history, the end of the class struggle, the end of philosophy, the death of God, the end of religions, the end of Christianity and morals . . ." Derrida, "Of an Apocalyptic Tone Recently Adopted in Philosophy," 69, 80. But as we shall see below, deconstruction could be said to be just as indebted to a Christian eschatology.

12. Caputo, "Apostles of the Impossible," 198.

or whether the specific particular histories of those religions are themselves "irreducible events" without which "we would not know what messianicity is." In impromptu remarks on this question, which occupied his attention on a number of occasions, Derrida notably concluded, "I confess that I hesitate between these two possibilities."[13]

And if there were any doubts that Hanson might have misrepresented Derrida's undecidability, Derrida himself laid those to rest when he conceded, at a conference held at Villanova University in 1997, that he shared Heidegger's similar difficulty over whether *Offenbarung* (revelation) or *Offenbarkeit* (the conditions of possibility for revelation) enjoys ontological primacy or priority; that is, the perennial question of whether structure or agency, or universality and historicity, or the chicken or the egg comes first.[14] Admitting to his own internal conflict over this Heideggerian problematic,[15] Derrida told his interlocutors, "That is why I am constantly really hesitating. That is part of—what can I call this here?—let us say, *my cross*."[16] One is here reminded of the case, in the gospel of Mark, of the father desperately seeking help for his demon-possessed son, who, when informed by Jesus that everything is possible for the one who believes, exclaimed by faith even as he acknowledged his dire need for divine help in his aporia: "I do believe; help me overcome my unbelief!" (Mark 9:24). At another conference also held at Villanova in 1999, Derrida again shared his struggle with indecision, admitting that "there is someone inside him who is constantly approving his actions and someone else who is very disapproving, even 'merciless' with him, and the two are 'constantly fighting'"[17]—a comment that bore a more than passing resemblance to Paul's description in Rom 7 of the dual natures, God's law and the law of sin, warring within

13. Hanson, "Tale of Two Doublets," 55.

14. Ware, "Universality and Historicity."

15. There is no question that Heidegger had a major influence over Derrida's work. As Derrida once observed about the hold Heidegger had over him, welcomed or otherwise: "For me, he is something like a watchman, a thinking that always keeps watch over me—an overseer who is always watching over me, a thinking that, I feel, has me under surveillance. For me, it is an inexhaustible relationship, which is made of, again, movements of positive admiration, of recognition, of debt and then, sometimes quite severely, of critical impatience, and always very ironic." Cited in Raffoul, "Heidegger and Derrida," 401.

16. Derrida's comments in his roundtable with Jean-Luc Marion and Richard Kearney in Kearney, "On the Gift," 73, italics mine.

17. Caputo, "What Do I Love When I Love My God?" 309.

himself. Indeed, the cross ostensibly borne by Derrida was one he steadfastly refused to lay down; crucially, Paul's remarkable statement that there is now "no condemnation for those who are in Christ Jesus," because he has set them free from the law of sin and death by the law of his Spirit (Rom 8:1–2), was not something Derrida likely experienced let alone embraced. As we shall see, a huge part of Derrida's burden or yoke had to do with his anxiety and fear over what the coming of Messiah might bring, including the prospect of a messiah that Derrida might not have really wanted, that he might find monstrous and terrifying, and that he would ultimately not know or be able to name.

Awaiting the Unwanted

In a telling extended conversation about deconstruction with John Caputo, Derrida's ruminations turned to religion and messianism, where he admitted to his fear over waiting for something or someone he would rather not wait for—the ultimate act of deferral and postponement—because he saw in the fulfillment of the messianic not life but death, something he did not welcome:

> But the Messiah might also be the one even while I do not want him to come. There is the possibility that my relation to the Messiah is this: I would like him to come, I hope that he will come, that the other will come, as other, for that would be justice, peace, and revolution—because in the concept of messianicity there is revolution—and, at the same time, I am scared. I do not want what I want and I would like the coming of the Messiah to be infinitely postponed, and there is this desire in me. That is why the man who addressed the Messiah said, "When will you come?" That is a way to say, well as long as I speak to you, as long as I ask you the question, "When will you come?" at least you are not coming. And that is the condition for me to go on asking questions and living. So there is some ambiguity in the messianic structure. *We wait for something we would not like to wait for. That is another name for death.*[18]

Derrida's reference above to the man who asked the Messiah, "When will you come?" drew upon an old rabbinic tradition once discussed by his friend Maurice Blanchot, who argued that the coming of Messiah should

---

18. Derrida, *Deconstruction in a Nutshell*, 24–25, italics mine.

not be confused with his actual presence.[19] For Derrida, even if Messiah were to show up and stand before him—presumably even at the second coming of Christ!—Derrida, like Blanchot, would *still* ask of him, "When will you come?"[20] For deconstruction, this is the very structure of what is meant by the Messiah: that if Messiah were to finally come—"I AM back!"—what would there be left to hope for? As Caputo explained, "For it belongs to the very idea of the Messiah to be always to come"[21]—*but never actually to come*. Here then is the paradox in which deconstruction finds itself: deconstruction lives for the coming of the Messiah, but it stays alive only insofar as Messiah never actually shows up. Derrida very much preferred to live than die. In the final interview Derrida gave before his passing in October 2004, he furnished this honest admission:

> No, I have never learned-to-live. In fact not at all! Learning to live should mean learning to die, learning to take into account, so as to accept, absolute mortality (that is, without salvation, resurrection, or redemption—neither for oneself nor for the other). That's been the old philosophical injunction since Plato: to philosophize is to learn to die. I believe in this truth without being able to resign myself to it. And less and less so. I have never learned to accept it, to accept death, that is.[22]

Perhaps it was Derrida's fear of facing a God from whom he could hide nothing, and the very thought of his whole existence being laid bare before a God who sees and knows everything—a "totalitarian" God—was more than he could bear. If he had his druthers, Derrida much preferred to keep his secrets secret. "I have a taste for the secret, it clearly has to do with not-belonging; I have an impulse or fear or terror in the face of a political space, for example, a public space that makes no room for the secret," as Derrida once confided to the Italian philosopher Maurizio Ferraris. "For me," he went on to explain, "the demand that everything be paraded in the

---

19. Blanchot's reflection on this issue, prompted by a commentary from one of Emmanuel Levinas's Talmudic writings, focused on the ambiguity surrounding the meaning of "today"—the answer the Messiah gave in reply to the question, "When will you come?" Leveraging on Levinas's discussion of Ps 95:7b—"*Today*, if only you would hear his voice"—Blanchot, among other things, reflected on whether "today" ought to be understood in chronological or in kairos (proper or opportune time) terms. Hill, *Maurice Blanchot and Fragmentary Writing*, 378–79.

20. Derrida, *Politics of Friendship*, 46n.

21. Caputo, "Apostles of the Impossible," 199.

22. Derrida, *Learning to Live Finally*, 24.

public square and that there be no internal forum is a glaring sign of the totalitarianization of democracy ... if a right to the secret is not maintained, we are in a totalitarian space."[23] Derrida's angst is not unusual; it is what haunts Christ-followers as well—if they are honest enough to admit it.[24] Does deconstruction's "waiting without waiting" effectively consign it to an incessant undecidability born of a desire, Derrida's desire to be precise, to continue living—and to eschew the death that ostensibly comes with Messiah come—as he saw it? But in a manner of speaking, Christ-followers who wait in anticipation for the Parousia of Christ—await without knowing the exact time of his return—intuitively understand and appreciate what Derrida was presumably referring to here, even if their wait is a wait *on* God (waiting on the God in whom they trust to fulfill his promises) as opposed to deconstruction's wait *for* God (of whom or what they know not and have no expectations), a point that the fourth chapter will further develop.

---

23. Cited in Peeters, *Derrida*, 511. Derrida evidently had his secrets or, as a commentator has put it, "second lives." Leitch, "Review: Excess." For example, it is well known that the married Derrida fathered a son with his mistress, the French philosopher Sylvaine Agacinski, in 1984. Reportedly, Agacinski insisted on having their child against Derrida's wishes. Derrida did not acknowledge his paternity until two years after the child (Daniel) was born, and only then at his wife Marguerite's urging, but he had no contact with his son Daniel. (Agacinski went on to marry the future Socialist Prime Minister of France, Lionel Jospin, who brought up Daniel as his own.) In his 1987 book *The Post Card*, Derrida wrote, presumably in oblique reference to his altercation with Agacinski over having their son, "To the devil with the child, the only thing we ever will have discussed, the child, the child, the child." Derrida, *Post Card*, 25. But there was another secret of his, one that he himself revealed in *Circumfession* where he wrote: " ... no doubt my writings can manifest but as though illegibly, following some rule of reading still to be formulated, is that 'I want to kill myself' is a sentence of mine, me all over, but known to me alone, the mise en scene of a suicide and the fictive but oh how motivated, convinced, serious decision to put an end to my days ..." Derrida, "Circumfession," 37–38.

24. As Mark Galli, the former editor-in-chief of *Christianity Today*, once admitted in his intensely personal reflection on the so-called "evangelical crisis" and his own felt need to have a greater love and deeper desire for God: "And that's when something occurred to me with great force: I wasn't sure I wanted that. I recognize that was an odd admission for a person who claimed to be a good Christian. But there it was. I didn't think I really wanted to love God more. The reasons for that are complex and will be touched on later, but the bottom line was: I really didn't want to love God." Galli, "Heart of the Evangelical Crisis."

Awaiting the Impossible

Awaiting the Monstrous

> What I mean is that when we control a border, when we try to discriminate, when we try to find criteria to discriminate between the enemy and the friend, *or between the monster and the god*, then the indispensable act of knowing, discriminating, adjusting the politics, is indispensable, no doubt, but it is in way of limiting hospitality . . . I'm not sure there is pure hospitality. But if we want to understand what hospitality means, we have to think of unconditional hospitality, that is, openness to whomever, to any newcomer. And of course, if I want to know in advance who is the good one, who is the bad one—in advance!—if I want to have an available criterion to distinguish between the good immigrant and the bad immigrant, then I would have no relation to the other as such. So to welcome the other as such, you have to suspend the use of criteria.[25]

Referencing Derrida's discussion of a potentially monstrous God to come, Caputo writes, "The figure of the future is an absolute surprise, and as such, Derrida says, something 'monstrous.' To prepare for the future, were it possible, would be to prepare for a coming species of monster, 'to welcome the monstrous *arrivant*, to welcome it, that is, to accord hospitality to that which is absolutely foreign and strange.' Whatever arrives as an 'event,' as an absolute surprise, first takes 'the form of the unacceptable, or even of the intolerable, of the incomprehensible, that is, of a certain monstrosity.'"[26] Remarkably, as we see in the epigraph above, Derrida insisted that hospitality for the unexpected visitor must necessarily be expansive enough to include room for an unwanted visitor—including monsters! Again, as he wrote in another place: "To wait without waiting, awaiting absolute surprise, the unexpected visitor, awaited without a horizon of expectation: this is indeed about the Messiah as *hôte*, about the messianic as hospitality, the messianic that introduces deconstructed disruption or madness in the concept of hospitality, the madness of hospitality, even the madness of the concept of hospitality," as Derrida wrote.[27] That is not to say that deconstruction views the welcoming of a monster an easy thing to do. Far from

---

25. Derrida in Kearney, "Desire of God," 132–33, italics mine.
26. Caputo, *Prayers and Tears of Jacques Derrida*, 74.
27. Derrida, "Hostipitality," 362. In this respect, Derrida was very much operating on the same terrain as Levinas's conception of hospitality as an infinite responsibility to the other.

it. Yet Derrida was uncompromising in his insistence that it had to be done: "I have always, consistently and insistently, held *unconditional hospitality*, as *impossible*, to be *heterogeneous* to the *political*, the *juridical*, and even the *ethical*."[28]

If there were biblical characters who faced the unexpected "monstrosity" of God, Job comes immediately to mind, he who faced overwhelming terrors—"What I feared has come upon me; what I dreaded has happened to me" (Job 3:25)—from the hand of Satan, granted, but permitted by God (Job 1:12; 2:6). The prophet Jeremiah went so far as to declare that he had been deceived by God (Jer 20:7). What enables such an indiscriminate hospitality toward even the monstrous and deceptive, for Derrida, is faith as he understood it: "If we refer to faith, it is to the extent that we don't see. Faith is needed when perception is lacking. I don't *see* the other, I don't *see* what he or she has in mind, or whether he or she wants to deceive me. So I have to trust the other, that is faith. Faith is blind."[29] What such blind faith—blind from the lack of revelation from an impossible God—also means is the readiness to accommodate even the monstrous. Yet it is noteworthy that for Job, Jeremiah, and other servants of God in similar predicaments, their faith was placed in their incomplete yet intimate knowledge of a loving and compassionate God who permitted difficult circumstances that ultimately work for their good (Rom 8:28).[30] As noted in the previous chapter, it was just such a conception of divine goodness that enabled Job, despite his state of abjection, to declare, perhaps more circumspectly but no less hopefully than the triumphant oratorio of Handel's *Messiah*: "I know that my redeemer lives, and that in the end he will stand on the earth. And after my skin has been destroyed, yet in my flesh I will see God; I myself will see him with my own eyes—I, and not another. How my heart yearns within me!" (Job 19:25–27). That Job could insist—seemingly against all hope, as Abraham, Paul, and other followers of the God of the Bible might say—that he *knew*, somehow, that his redeemer lives implies that the utmost monstrosity that confronted and overwhelmed him did not completely obliterate his memory of his lived experience of God's goodness. That biblical faith

---

28. Derrida, *Rogues*, 172 n.2, italics original.

29. Derrida, *Questioning Ethics*, 80, italics original.

30. Arguably, the knowledge we can have of God grows as we press into seeking and knowing him, but it is never a complete knowledge because God himself limits his revelations: "The secret things belong to the Lord our God, but the things revealed belong to us and to our children forever, that we may follow all the words of this law" (Deut 29:29).

is arguably knowledgeable rather than totally blind is elaborated in the next section.

Awaiting the Unknown(able)

Is there no room at all within deconstruction for received revelation about what one could expect of the coming Messiah? Has God stayed completely silent on his personality, purposes, and plans? And yet we are told in Amos 3:7 that God does nothing without revealing his plan to his servants the prophets. As Richard Kearney has mused, if the impossible God that deconstruction awaits and welcomes is a "*tout autre* without face" and an "impossible, unimaginable, unforeseeable, unbelievable absolute surprise," how can we even be expected to trust fully in "a God devoid of all names" and in "a faith devoid of stories and covenants, promises, alliances, and good works," that leaves us "without vision, without truth, without revelation"?[31] The intention of deconstruction to avoid idolatry through an emphatic insistence on God as truly absolute and wholly other (*tout autre*) is understandable, even admirable. However, if human beings are made in the likeness of God (Gen 1:27)—and here I borrow Wolfhart Pannenberg's notion of *imago Dei* as "the human destination to communion with God"[32]—it raises the question whether we can even commune with God under the conditions of deconstruction's *tout autre*, which rejects the possibility of any knowledge of God or the memory of such. In his comparative analysis of the questions that both Job (e.g., "Why do you hide your face and consider me your enemy?"; Job 13:24) and Augustine ("What then do I love when I love my God?" in *The Confessions*) had for God, Graham Ward argued that far as both those inquirers were concerned, their questions were posed within the context of their respective relationships with God, without which their queries would likely not have been possible:

> We must observe here that for Job and Augustine, the other is neither just otherness nor, in being alterior, even wholly other (*tout autre*). For the relationship to be a relationship, a history of practiced believing is required, the memory (one's own and one's communities') of past engagement, past epiphany, past revelations . . . Augustine may doubt his knowledge of what God is, and Job may be confused by this activity as God's activity; nevertheless,

---

31. Kearney, "Desire of God," 126–27.
32. Pannenberg, *Anthropology in Theological Perspective*, 74.

the entrustment, hope, and assurance that makes their questioning possible is found upon this memory of past engagement in which *that* which they name God has been demonstrated to be faithful. The *tout autre* as such puts an end to all revelation and inaugurates a discourse of ineliminable yet impossible and undecidable trace.[33]

To my mind, nowhere is Ward's point about the memory of past engagements, epiphanies, and revelations more evident than in the book of Lamentations (ascribed by tradition as the work of the prophet Jeremiah), whose author's double remembering of his (and Israel's) woes, on the one hand, and God's great love and faithfulness on the other, argues for the possibility of some knowledge of God, incomplete thought it be:

> I remember my affliction and my wandering, the bitterness and the gall. I well remember them, and my soul is downcast within me. *Yet this I call to mind and therefore I have hope*: Because of the Lord's great love we are not consumed, for his compassions never fail. They are new every morning; great is your faithfulness. I say to myself, "The Lord is my portion; therefore I will wait for him." The Lord is good to those whose hope is in him, to the one who seeks him; it is good to wait quietly for the salvation of the Lord (Lam 3:19–26, italics mine).

How could the author here insist that the Lord is good to those who hope in him—and who therefore are willing to wait in anticipation for the salvation promised them—unless the author held some prior knowledge of the ostensible goodness of his God? We will return to this crucial point about the otherness of God in the final chapter.

For Derrida, however, even the very idea of naming and labelling proved challenging for him as it meant the violent attempt to capture something that always eludes its grasp: "My instinct has always been to flee, as if, at first contact, just by *naming* these concepts, I was going to find myself, like the fly, with my legs trapped in glue: captive, paralyzed, a hostage, trapped by a program."[34] Accordingly, the condition of absolute surprise and absolute impossibility must adhere because that would be in all good conscience the just and honest thing to do. Otherwise, "One might as well give up also on whatever good conscience one still claims to preserve. One might as well confess the economic calculation and declare all

---

33. Ward, "Questioning God," 276–77.
34. Cited in Peeters, *Derrida*, 490.

the checkpoints that ethics, hospitality, or the various messianisms would still install at the borders of the event in order to screen the *arrivant*."[35] For deconstruction, no news about or from the Messiah is good news. There can be no news, good or bad, because the logic of deconstruction, to use Philippe Lacoue Labarthe's terms, "is, rigorously speaking, the *interdiction of revelation*."[36] That said, for deconstruction, no news does not mean it thereby awaits something that is really nothing; it is just that it does not quite know what to expect—it is not only unknown but unknowable. "But the impossible is not nothing," as Derrida sought to explain. "It is even that which happens, which comes, by definition. I admit that this remains rather difficult to think, but that's exactly what preoccupies thinking, if there is any and from the time there is any."[37] Indeed, Derrida seemed to think there could ultimately be no answers to the questions he posed, since no revelation from the *tout autre* would, in his mind, ever be conceivable.[38] And if one does not quite know what to expect, one therefore cannot really know how one would react either, if or when the impossible finally shows up.[39]

Seen in the context of Derrida's apparent preference for an indefinite postponement or deferral of the Messiah's coming, it underscores his sense of undecidability motivated perhaps by unnamed anxieties and fears.[40] Viewed from the Christian perspective, Derrida's apparent refusal to take a (Kierkegaardian) leap of faith about faith—because he sought life rather than death—leads to a potentially tragic situation. Leveraging on Hélène

---

35. Derrida, *Specters of Marx*, 81–82.
36. Labarthe, *Typography*, 118, italics mine.
37. Derrida, *Rogues*, 172n.
38. Derrida, *Post Card*.

39. As Derrida put it, "We should not pretend to know what trembling means, to know what it means really to tremble, since trembling will always remain heterogeneous to knowledge ... The experience of trembling is always the experience of an absolute passivity, absolutely exposed, absolutely vulnerable, passive in the face of an unpredictable future. Shuddering can, to be sure, be a demonstration of fear, anxiety, the apprehension of death, when one shudders in advance at the idea of what is going to happen. But it can be light, on the surface of the skin, when shuddering announces pleasure or ecstasy." Cited in Peeters, *Derrida*, 533.

40. Deconstructionists such as William Connolly have raised concerns, expressed in different contexts, about the proclivity of his colleagues to remain indefinitely in their undecidability. Connolly, *William E. Connolly: Democracy, Pluralism and Political Theory*, 220.

Cixous's description of Derrida as a "Jewish saint,"[41] Victor Taylor made this acute comparison between Derrida's sense of expectancy, as marked by his sad jocularity (hence "Jacques-ularity" below, per Taylor's pun), and that of Sarah in the Genesis narrative, she who laughed at the impossibility of God's remarkable promise of a son she would bear in her old age:

> This "Jacques-ularity," one could say, is the opposite of Sarah's laughter insofar as Sarah laughed at "infinite" impossibility and Derrida seems to laugh at 'infinite possibility.' St. Derrida, then, the jocular saint, keeps us apart, does not sound, as others would, the call for us to be bound to something. Instead, St. Derrida draws us toward laughter and binds us to nothing but the infinitely divisible point, bearing witness, finally, to his inability to bear witness, to stop his sad laughter without end.[42]

An incessant mirth like that exhibited by deconstruction that is unbounded, which allows only what is humanly possible—with Christ already ruled out, unless that falls within the realm of Derrida's "infinitely possible"—might seem a rather unfocused and myopic endeavor for accessing the holy. And is that so surprising a conclusion for one who once confessed he was but "the slave of an infinite" whom he did not understand and a wanderer "in the desert of deconstruction which [would] never announce the truth"?[43]

Deciding Amid Undecidability

The foregoing discussion leads to another key concern: Given its indefinite undecidability, how is deconstruction able at all to dismiss the biblical Jesus as Messiah, if indeed it has done so? Over several reflections where he sought to distinguish between law, justice, and ethics,[44] Derrida made a powerful case for decisions that are rendered within the context of undecidability, as opposed to the conventional understanding of decision-making in the mold, say, of Carl Schmitt's realpolitik or strongman notion of decisionism, which could be understood as a decisive judgment that forces a resolution to, a reconciliation of, the tension of aporia.[45] Rather, the toughest deci-

---

41. Cixous, *Portrait of Jacques Derrida as A Young Jewish Saint*.
42. Taylor, "Divisible Derridas," 3.
43. Wright, "Through a *Glas* Darkly," 73.
44. Derrida in "Force of Law" and *The Gift of Death*, inter alia.
45. Mouffe, *Challenge of Carl Schmitt*.

sions are those made in difficult or even impossible circumstances; indeed, Derrida would say that many if not most of our decisions are rendered in various conditions of aporia and undecidability. And lest we imagine deconstruction's undecidability is the opposite of a decision, Derrida would insist that undecidability is more properly the condition of possibility of a decision—not unlike, as we saw in the previous chapter, Derrida's (via Kierkegaard's) reflection on Abraham's sacrifice of Isaac. As Caputo has noted elsewhere, Derrida would constantly bring up the issue of the undecidability of situations and the complications that beset any decision but insist that at a certain point deliberation must cease and a decision needs to be taken.[46] Much like his insistence that the gift, if it were to be truly a gift, must exceed the bounds of economy, Derrida argued that a decision would not be an ethical decision if it could be calculated, programmed, or deduced from some universal law.[47] As Caputo has explained Derrida's reasoning:

> [T]he opposite of "undecidability" is not "decisiveness" but programmability, calculability, computerizability, or formalizability. Decision-making, judgment, on the other hand, positively *depends* on undecidability . . . So a "just" decision, a "judgment" that is worthy of the name, one that responds to the demands of justice, one that is more than merely legal, goes eyeball to eyeball with undecidability, stares it in the face (literally), looks into the abyss, and then makes the leap, that is "gives itself up to the impossible decision." . . . That does not mean it is "decisionistic," for that would break the tension in the opposite direction, by dropping or ignoring the law altogether and substituting subjectivistic autonomy for responsibility to the other.[48]

Decisions rendered amid extremely difficult and complex situations are part and parcel of the life of faith. Here we are reminded of Job's three friends and their unwarranted exaggeration of the principle that God's faithful and obedient servants are always blessed, and anything else to the contrary automatically implies they are being punished by God for their sin (e.g., Job 8:1–7). Arguably, Eliphaz, Bildad, and Zophar represent those who would rather eschew the ambiguities posed by a life of faith in God and rely uncritically on the certitude of warmed-over formulas, and for whom

---

46. Caputo, "Power of the Powerless," 139.
47. Derrida, "Force of Law."
48. Derrida and Caputo, "Justice, If Such a Thing Exists," 137.

the idea of giving themselves over to the "impossible decision" highlighted by Derrida (and Kierkegaard before him) is completely foreign. Elsewhere Kevin Hart, thinking along the same lines, has suggested that faith "is an opening of experience, one that must be reaffirmed in its irresolvable tension so long as it is lived; and if it is not lived—risked, challenged—it is not faith at all but merely a sacred code."[49] Or perhaps, to paraphrase Chesterton, the life of faith had been found wanting by Job's friends and thereby left untried, so comfortable and secure they were participating in their "sacred codes." Indeed, their attitudes and actions reflect injustice toward not only Job but also God as well; "I am angry with you [Eliphaz] and your two friends, because you have not spoken the truth about me, as my servant Job has" (Job 42:7). Understood from this vantage, the commitment to decide amid undecidability implies that deconstruction is not an invitation to paralysis. Deconstruction does not aim to reduce us to the "underground man" in Dostoevsky's *Notes from Underground*, whose hyper-consciousness caused him to be indecisive, doubtful, and overly self-critical, always questioning things around him but doing little else of worth. Rather, deconstruction brings a healthy dose of agnosticism and self-irony to its watchful pursuit of the holy and the messianic through situating the seeker between the promise of God's presence and its impossibility[50]—because, to borrow from Robert Browning's poem "Rabbi Ben Ezra," the best, far as deconstruction is concerned, is always yet to be. Graham Ward insists (correctly in my view) that Derrida's agnosticism—his "irreducible openness to the trace of a promise" that steadfastly refuses to assign the trace under a particular religious tradition or to accommodate it under the name and sign of a specific messiah—is not to be confused with faith, if by that we mean a commitment to the God of the Bible.[51]

That said, Ward also suggested that faith is the supplementary movement that comes, if it is permitted to come at all, beyond the point of deconstruction's hesitation at the threshold of decision and effectively arresting its endless questioning.[52] But this was *not* how Derrida saw it. As we noted a few pages ago, for deconstruction, the entire experience with undecidability from beginning to end is to be negotiated through *blind*

---

49. Hart, "Absolute Interruption," 197.
50. Ward, *Barth, Derrida and the Language of Theology*, 232–33.
51. Ward, *Barth, Derrida and the Language of Theology*, 251.
52. Caputo, "What Do I Love When I Love My God?" 295.

faith in the wholly other.[53] It is not as if faith allows one to overcome undecidability and leave it behind; rather, undecidability persists as the context in which faith continually lives—or, in Derrida's words, "The aporia is the experience of responsibility."[54] Perhaps it could be said that deconstruction's own movement of faith consists in a repetitive alternation of response and retreat vis-à-vis messianic prospects, leaning toward them but all the while maintaining a certain ironic distance from them, not unlike a sailboat tacking back and forth in the wind between points it aims for but never quite reaches. "Rather, it means that we are always responding and at the same always asking what we are responding to, always choosing and at the same asking what we have chosen or has chosen us, what we are doing in the midst of the concrete decisions we always and invariably make," as Caputo has put it. "We are, just as he [Derrida] says in 'Circumfession,' always asking what do I love when I love my God? Deconstruction is not a philosophy of undecidability *tout court*, but of deciding-in-the-midst-of-undecidability . . ."[55] Absent undecidability, there could be no decision or responsibility or faith. In this respect, perhaps it could also be said that Derrida's impossible decision, as we have seen, is determined by a level of self-imposed impossibility that *exceeds* that which confronted Abraham:

> Here it isn't a matter of knowing what the other knows, for Abraham doesn't know anything. It isn't a matter of sharing his faith, for the latter must remain an initiative of absolute singularity. And moreover, we don't think or speak of Abraham from the point of view of a faith that is sure of itself, any more than did Kierkegaard

---

53. Derrida, *Questioning Ethics*, 80.

54. From Derrida's comments in Kearney, "On Forgiveness," 62. Derrida went on to say in that same statement: "If I know what I have to do, if I know in advance what has to be done, then there is no responsibility. For the responsible decision to be envisaged or taken, we have to go through pain and aporia, a situation in which I do not know what to do." Kearney, "On Forgiveness," 62.

55. In a manner of speaking, the question for Derrida and deconstruction is neither the existence of God nor even whether we love God for that matter, but, with the Augustinian emphasis that so affected and delighted Derrida: *What* do we love when we love *our* God? *What*—because what we believe has to do with our deepest desires and loves—and *our*—because the "God" for whom or which Derrida was waiting is not (necessarily) the Christ of the Bible. Ganssle, *Our Deepest Desires*, 4. As Caputo noted, "For there are many things that we might mean by God and many things that we might confuse with God—such as our own ego, our own will, our own pleasures, our own opinions, our own religion, our own nation—all of which are very good at masquerading under the name of God. So everything depends upon what we love when we love our God." Caputo, "What Do I Love When I Love My God?" 291–92.

> . . . Our faith is not assured because a faith never can be, it must never be a certainty. We share with Abraham what cannot be shared, a secret we know nothing about, neither him nor us. To share a secret is not to know or to reveal the secret, it is to share we know not what: nothing that can be known, nothing that can be determined.[56]

And yet, as we saw in the preceding chapter (and as the Genesis account would attest), Abraham did not operate from a state of absolute ignorance. Given his relationship with God, one based on an incomplete but no less intimate knowledge of the God who called him, Abraham acted out of hope in the assurances and promises of the Other—the God who had not only spoken to him specific words but took him out of his tent to ponder the starry night sky as a visual aid (Gen 15:5)—whom he deemed reliable and trustworthy. But nowhere and not once did Abraham's hopeful conduct nullify the need for faith; rather, they went hand in glove. As the writer of Hebrews has put it, "faith is confidence in what we hope for and assurance about what we do not see. This is what the ancients were commended for" (Heb 11:1–2). In this sense, what I have referred to as an extant knowledge of God does not exist independent of faith in God but is in fact dependent on it. Accordingly, faith is not a supplement or an adjunct to knowledge; rather, faith drives the quest for knowledge and is driven by it[57]—or, to borrow from Anselm, "faith seeking understanding" (*fides quaerens intellectum*). In a sense, Derrida was quite right to insist that faith is the be-all-and-end-all of everything.[58]

Nevertheless, far as Derrida were concerned, Abraham, for all intents and purposes, "had even renounced hope."[59] What seems absent from Derrida's logic here is any sense of what it was that conceivably motivated Abraham to decide and act the way he did. As the writer of Hebrews put it, "By faith Abraham, when God tested him, offered Isaac as a sacrifice. He who had embraced the promises was about to sacrifice his one and only son, even though God had said to him, 'It is through Isaac that your

---

56. Derrida, *Gift of Death*, 79–80.

57. That said, I hope nonetheless to avoid the so-called Nietzschean trap of "metalepsis"—that is, the fallacy of substituting an effect for a cause and vice versa, when thinking in causal terms. Williams, "Metaphysics and Metalepsis."

58. In this respect, Volf and Croasmun have gone to the point of insisting, "Theology is the practice of *pilgrims seeking understanding*—and anyone else who may want to listen." Volf and Croasmun, *For the Life of the World*, 121, italics original.

59. Derrida, *Gift of Death*, 72.

offspring will be reckoned.' *Abraham reasoned that God could even raise the dead*, and so in a manner of speaking he did receive Isaac back from death" (Heb 11:17–19, italics mine). Likewise, referring to Abraham's faith in the divine promise of both natural and spiritual fatherhood despite his (and Sarah's) aged condition, Paul wrote, "Against all hope, Abraham in hope believed . . ." (Rom 4:18). The hope that enabled Abraham to believe was in something or someone from out of this world, since all hope of worldly origins and in worldly possibilities, by Paul's account, no longer existed for Abraham. By contrast, Derrida's Abraham was a man completely *without* hope, whose conduct was born purely out of obligation without room for reasoning and rationalization, which for Derrida are logics that remain within the economy of calculation and hence questionable: "Abraham had consented to suffer death or worse, and that without calculating, without investing, beyond any perspective of recouping the loss; hence, it seems, beyond recompense or retribution, beyond economy, without any hope of remuneration [*solaire*]."[60]

Granted, Paul's declaration in 1 Tim 1:12—"I know whom I have believed, and am convinced that he is able to guard what I have entrusted to him until that day"—and others like it seem to imply a kind of bounded rationality at work, where the Christian's walk of faith deepens daily with—and, in a practical sense, depends on—increasing knowledge of and intimacy with her God.[61] But while that knowledge conceivably contrib-

60. Derrida, *Gift of Death*, 95. Without saying as much, Caputo's perspective on the question of hopefulness and hopelessness, at least indirectly in Abraham's context—as well as Paul's notion of "hope against hope" in Rom 4:18—seems to differ somewhat from that of Derrida. As Caputo has noted, "Undecidability does not undo faith, hope, and love but provides them with their condition of possibility, supplying their element, the night in which they are formed and performed. Faith is faith just when things are starting to look a little incredible and unlikely, even as faith vanishes entirely under the sun of knowledge. Faith is faith when it holds out against the voices of disbelief that grow stronger and stronger, voices from within and without, when it holds on even as the evidence against it mounts up. You have believed because you saw, Thomas, but blessed are those who believe and have not seen (John 20:29). Hope is really hope just when things are starting to look hopeless, when the odds are mounting up against us, when reasonable people would cut their losses and head for cover. *Hope is hope, as St. Paul said in a magnificent formulation, when it is hope against hope* (Rom 4:18)." Caputo, "What Do I Love When I Love My God?" 313–14, italics mine. Perhaps my suggested distinction between Caputo and Derrida is erroneous or exaggerated and hence negligible, but that said, Caputo, much like Derrida, would probably not wish to make much of the place of knowledge and memory in Abraham's thinking that guided his faith-based attempt to sacrifice Isaac, at least per Paul's explanation in Heb 11:19.

61. For an interesting take on the impact of bounded rationality on the giving of

utes to reason and rationality, it is just as likely to confound commonsense and militate against any wrongful application of past experiences and revelations, especially where old knowledge contradicts or contravenes new knowledge from God: think, for instance, of Moses striking the rock for water instead of speaking to it in the Desert of Zin, as God had instructed, because Moses, among other things, was relying on prior knowledge whose "use by date" had passed (Num 20:1–13; Exod 17:1–7). Returning to Dostoevsky's *Notes from Underground*, reason knows only what it has managed to learn, and humankind as such can never be confined to reason at the expense of its free agency—nor, for our purposes here, faith. Christian faith is about viewing through a glass darkly (1 Cor 12:4), but unlike deconstruction's Messiah of whom nothing can ever be known, the God of Abraham, Isaac, and Jacob, who covenants, walks, and talks with his people, is different than Derrida's impossible God of whom or which nothing can be known.

Given Derrida's charge against Kierkegaard for Christianizing his analysis of the Abraham and Isaac story in Gen 22,[62] deconstruction's "failure" to consider the biblical explanation is understandable. Instead of a Kierkegaardian leap of faith toward Christ, we see in deconstruction the possibility of a different leap of faith taking place within the context of undecidability. I suggest that deconstruction, despite its declared openness to all messianic possibilities, has rendered what amounts practically to a sort of metaphysical closure (or something close to it) against the prospect of the biblical Jesus as Messiah. The decision does not adopt the form of a decisionism that forcibly resolves or reconciles the tension of aporia, but it arises almost inexorably from the conditions of revealability which deconstruction has set for itself, namely, its hermeneutic of suspicion against all existing messianic and eschatological claims including the gospel. It is, to borrow from Heidegger, a sort of "Offenbarkeit moment" for deconstruction, where, despite deconstruction's undecidability, a *pragmatic* decision against Christology has in fact been taken and continues to be maintained, for all intents and purposes. As Kevin Hart has observed concerning Derrida's conception of faith awaiting Messiah's coming:

> Faith is not to be accommodated in Christology; indeed, since faith, *croyance*, eschews prediction, it is not to be accommodated

---

tithes and offerings, see, Hoffman, Lott, and Jeppsen, "Religious Giving and the Boundedness of Rationality."

62. Derrida, *Learning to Live Finally*, 50–51.

anywhere. Yet what Derrida retains from Kant is something older than the liberalization of faith. I am thinking of Jesus's preaching of the kingdom, which started to attract attention only with the Enlightenment. For Kant, the kingdom was to be understood in purely ethical terms, and this thought has remained in play in theology for the past two centuries, even when the kingdom has come to be interpreted by way of eschatology, even apocalypse. The *basileia* [kingdom] for Derrida is not an eschatological reign of God; it has no parousia as horizon; it is unequal to itself and is always "to come" (*á venir*) rather than abiding in a future present (*l'avenir*).[63]

That deconstruction is waiting for a kingdom not of Christ implies a decision *against Christ* has already been rendered amid deconstruction's undecidability.

Deciding Against Christ?

If Derridean deconstruction has effectively decided against Christ, what might the basis for its apparent objection against Christology be? What might deconstruction point to as the purported facts of orthodox Christianity's so-called "idolatry" in privileging the biblical Jesus? For one thing, its suspicion against the claim that faith can be predicated upon historically contingent and irreducible events—most crucially, the death, burial, and resurrection of Christ. Stated baldly, Jesus Christ is a historically specific determination, and his followers are viewed by deconstruction as having cast their lot with a specific messianism, one with a proper name and historical determinacy.[64] In Derrida's view, the messianic "has no need of the event of a revelation or the revelation of an event. It needs to think the possibility of such an event but not the event itself."[65] He essentially resisted the notion that the Christian mystery could be reduced to the absolute singularity of specific historical events[66]—although, as we saw earlier, he also professed his hesitancy over the messianic as either universal in kind or a particular event. Indeed, in another place he seemingly privileged the particular in describing the messianic as "the coming of the

---

63. Hart, "Absolute Interruption," 188.
64. Caputo, "What Do I Love When I Love My God?" 297.
65. Derrida, *Gift of Death*, 49.
66. Derrida, *Gift of Death*, 2; also see, Raschke and Hale, "Not Your Grandmother's Theory of Religion."

other, the absolute and unpredictable singularity of the *arrivant as justice*."[67] Beyond that philosophical objection, the possibility that Derrida could have regarded the empirical facticity of the nativity and passion of Christ as dubious and therefore unbelievable cannot be ruled out.[68] On this point, Derrida would be in good company with, say, Rudolf Bultmann or even John Shelby Spong (the former bishop of the American Episcopal Church), who likewise dismissed the virgin birth and/or the resurrection as myths of the early Church in their respective efforts to demythologize Christianity.[69] Nor could we rule out the possibility that Derrida, like many other Jewish thinkers before him (even though Judaism for him constituted one of the concrete messianisms), likely did not accept the dual covenant perspective which sees Judaism and Christianity playing complementary if not cooperative roles together.[70] For example, Franz Rosenzweig once argued that the Christian emphasis on Jesus Christ as the only intermediary through which God-seekers can access the Father (in John 14:6) is, for Rosenzweig, invalidated by the argument that it is different for the Jewish people because the Father is already with them.[71]

Furthermore, Derrida's hesitation to locate the messianic in Christology can also be attributed to deconstruction's skepticism toward all forms

---

67. Derrida, *Specters of Marx*, 33.

68. In *Specters of Marx*, Derrida took umbrage with Francis Fukuyama's end-of-history thesis in the latter's *The End of History and the Last Man*, which, in Derrida's judgment, fails the empirical test. According to Derrida, since Fukuyama could not deny the violence and injustices that comprise a big part of the capitalist world of imperfect liberal democracies—as he put it, "no degree of progress allows one to ignore that never before, in absolute figures, never have so many men, women, and children been subjugated, starved, or exterminated on the earth" (*Specters of Marx*, 106)—Fukuyama was therefore unable to announce the end of history as "*de facto* good news" but resorted to presenting it as "an *ideal* good news, the teleo-eschatological good news, which is inadequate to any empiricity," or democracy indefinitely deferred. As Derrida concluded, "That is why we always propose to speak of a democracy *to come*, not of a *future* democracy in the future present, not even of a regulating idea, in the Kantian sense, or of a utopia – at least to the extent that their inaccessibility would still retain the temporal form of a *future present*, of a future modality of the *living present*." Derrida, *Specters of Marx*, 80–81. In view of his critique of Fukuyama's end-of-history as a Christian eschatology, one wonders if Derrida might not have felt that Christianity has yet to prove it can (in his words) "respect its own promise" through fulfillment. Derrida, *Specters of Marx*, 131.

69. Bultmann, *New Testament Mythology and Other Basic Writings*, and Spong, *Resurrection: Myth or Reality?*

70. Sigal, "Aspects of Dual Covenant Theology."

71. Schwarzschild, *Franz Rosenzweig*, 31–36.

of teleology, as opposed to eschatology, because of their proclivity to totalize—to conclude and delimit—*in advance*, thereby foreclosing possibilities unanticipated by their given telos. For Derrida, there is a clear distinction between teleology and eschatology. The former has clearly assigned and identified objectives and destinations and mapped-out paths toward their realization. The latter (as he understood it) leaves both destination and path open-ended and undefined. As he once mused:

> If that's possible, *if there is any* future, but how can one suspend such a question or deprive oneself of such a reserve without *concluding in advance*, without reducing in advance both the future and its chance? Without totalizing in advance? We must discern here between eschatology and teleology, even if the stakes of such a difference risk constantly being effaced in the most fragile and slight insubstantiality—and will be in a certain way always and necessarily deprived of any insurance against this risk. Is there not a messianic extremity, an *eskhaton* whose ultimate event (immediate rupture, unheard-of interruption, untimeliness of the infinite surprise, heterogeneity without accomplishment) can exceed, *at each moment*, the final term of a *phusis*, such as work, the production, and the *telos* of any history?[72]

He further explained his suspicions with any declared eschatology that, for all intents and purposes, is in fact a totalizing teleology—and it is evident he included Christian eschatology in this category—because of its ahistorical essence:

> Not in order to oppose it with an end of history or an ahistoricity, but, on the contrary, in order to show that this onto-theo-archeo-teleology locks up, neutralizes, and finally cancels historicity. It was then a matter of thinking another historicity—not a new history or still less a "new historicism," but another opening of event-ness as historicity that permitted one not to renounce, but on the contrary to open up access to an affirmative thinking of the messianic and emancipatory promise as promise: as *promise* and not as onto-theological or teleo-eschatological program or design. Not only must one not renounce the emancipatory desire, it is necessary to insist on it more than ever, it seems, and insist on it, moreover, as the very indestructibility of the "it is necessary."[73]

---

72. Derrida, *Specters of Marx*, 45, italics original.
73. Derrida, *Specters of Marx*, 95.

Awaiting Deconstruction's Impossible God

If the preaching of Christ crucified is a stumbling block to Jews and foolishness to Gentiles (1 Cor 1:23), then the fundamental, nonnegotiable, and irreducible singularity of the incarnate Christ—his life, death, and resurrection—in the gospel arguably offends deconstruction's sensibilities about the dangers of totalizing teleology. As Elaine Pagels asked, "Why does faith in the passion and death of Christ become an essential element—some say, *the* essential element—of orthodox Christianity?"[74] To both Pagel's and Derrida's concerns, we might offer Barth's memorable statement: "A Christianity that is not wholly eschatology and nothing but eschatology has absolutely nothing to do with Christ."[75] Or this equally emphatic statement from Karl Rahner: "*Christ* himself is the hermeneutical principle of all eschatological assertions. Anything that cannot be read and understood as a christological assertion is not a genuine eschatological assertion."[76] That said, Derrida was surely not incorrect to dismiss Christian eschatology as teleology in drag so long as it remains stuck in its "incorrigible Platonism," where the conceptual capture and abstraction of God as a category of substance, as a fixed presence or essence, ends up divesting eschatology—all expressions of eschatology, to be sure, but especially the Christian eschaton—of its connection with covenantal promise and relationship.[77] For instance, it has been argued that the exchange between God and Moses at the burning bush—"God said to Moses, 'I AM WHO I AM. This is what you are to say to the Israelites: "I AM has sent me to you"'" (Exod 3:14)—is better understood as a divine solicitation that invites, that summons, the human to a covenantal alliance with God "toward an eschatological horizon," more so than a metaphysical imperative.[78] Christian audiences would do well to remember that their own inherited eschatology is not a prefixed teleology but a protean journey with the divine Other, a walkabout full of unexpected surprises with the accent on *becoming* rather than being. Indeed, if Derrida took umbrage with a seemingly capricious God for coercing Abraham toward filicide as a test of his faith—from which, as we saw earlier, Derrida concluded Christianity is therefore unable to thematize responsibility—then is it not possible for us to read the burning bush episode as the

---

74. Pagels, *Gnostic Gospels*, 75, italics original.
75. Barth, *Epistle to the Romans*, 314.
76. Rahner, "Hermeneutics of Eschatological Assertions," 342, italics original.
77. Horton, *Covenant and Eschatology*.
78. Kearney, "God Who May Be," 157.

inauguration of "a new mode of divine relation" between God and man,[79] where God informed the Hebrews that he had witnessed their misery in Egypt and promised to rescue and deliver them to "a land flowing with milk and honey" (Exod 3:16–17)? Could this not be read as a sort of divine correction to—or if you like, a progressive revelation about—the character of God from that initially deduced by Derrida? We will revisit this theme of a God who covenants, talks, and walks with his people, a conception so unlike deconstruction's impossible God, in the next chapter.

Thinking Christ Hypothetically

If he were at all to consider the biblical Jesus as the Messiah for whom he had been waiting, Derrida seemed to prefer a noncorporeal Christ; there is, if you will, a hint of the gnostic in his thinking on this because Jesus, for Derrida, was the greatest and most incomprehensible of ghosts.[80] "Christ is the most spectral of specters. He tells us something about absolute spectrality," as Derrida once mused.[81] An unseen God is therefore, for Derrida, an inaccessible messiah whose paralyzing gaze evokes a mixture of dread, fear, and trembling.[82] Recall, as discussed in the previous chapter, that Derrida took issue with the Christian God for his purported invisibility and inaccessibility—the *mysterium tremendum*, who transfixes his followers with his gaze—who sees even what they do in secret, but without himself being visible or accessible.[83] Yet nowhere does deconstruction consider Jesus's claim, "Anyone who has seen me has seen the Father" (John 14:9). Rather than God hiding from us, it is we who hide from him, as Adam and Eve sought vainly to do among the trees in the Garden (Gen 3:8–10).

But this still begs the question: Why should deconstruction fear an invisible God, if indeed that were the case? After all, does not deconstruction await an impossible God, one devoid of face, name, story, covenant, vision, revelation[84]—in short, an unknown (and unknowable) and unnamed (and unnamable) God, an *Agnōstos Theos*? Christ is the most spectral of

---

79. LaCocque, "Revelation of Revelations," 315.

80. Goldman, "Christian Mystery and Responsibility Gnosticism," and Taylor, "Jesus' Spectral Intervention."

81. Derrida, *Specters of Marx*, 144.

82. Derrida, *Gift of Death*, 33.

83. Derrida, *Gift of Death*, 25.

84. As argued in Kearney, "Desire of God."

specters, the ghost of all ghosts, so Derrida claimed; the disciples who saw him walking on the lake and thinking him a ghost might not be wont to disagree (Matt 14:26)! To that, Mike Mason offers this intriguing rejoinder: "God has no desire to conceal Himself; on the contrary His desire is for full self-disclosure. The real problem is that people hide themselves from God, and God has to go looking for them (see Gen. 3:8–10). *So it is not God who is the ghost, but man.*"[85] But even if we were to allow Derrida's claim, could Jesus not then be the unexpected visitor and monstrous *arrivant* which deconstruction ought to hospitably accommodate? If there were any chance of this happening at all, likely it would have occurred within the context of what Derrida once called "something in excess of knowledge." Let us return to Derrida's insistence that a gift can only truly be a gift when it transgresses the economy of calculation, limitation, and reciprocity, if it exceeds those bounds.[86] In his rejoinder to a presentation given by Jean-Luc Marion, Derrida offered this thought on the possibility of thought: "The gift, I would claim, I would argue, as such cannot be known; as soon as you know it, you destroy it. So the gift as such is impossible . . . *The gift as such cannot be known, but it can be thought of. We can think what we cannot know* . . . But there is something in excess of knowledge."[87] That the gift is unknowable but not unthinkable constitutes an intriguing concession. For Derrida, his insistence that the gift is unknowable presumably led him to reject the concrete determinate messianisms and claims of singularly irreducible historical events like the nativity and passion of Christ.

But in allowing for the possibility of thought—by suggesting that the unknowability of the gift does not preclude one's reflection on its possibility, because, "We can think what we cannot know"—one wonders, given Derrida's obvious admiration for Kierkegaard's work even as he critiqued the latter's Christian commitment,[88] if Derrida did not have in mind Kierkegaard's rumination about Hegel's "arrogant" philosophy.[89] As

---

85. Mason, *Gospel According to Job*, 117.

86. Jacques Derrida, *Given Time*, 91.

87. Derrida in Kearney, "On the Gift," 60, italics mine.

88. According to Derrida, "*The Gift of Death* was meant to be, among many other things . . . an attempt to give another reading of Kierkegaard's Abraham. Despite my enormous admiration for this thinker, I tried to show that he perhaps Christianized the story of the binding of Isaac." Derrida, *Learning to Live Finally*, 50–51.

89. That said, Hanson interestingly has argued that Kierkegaard—or certainly Derrida's critique of Kierkegaard's Christology in, say, the latter's reading of Abraham's sacrifice of Isaac in *Fear and Trembling*—is not really the principal point of Derrida's effort.

Kierkegaard wrote, "If Hegel had written the whole of his logic and then said, in the preface or some other place, that it was merely an experiment in thought in which he had even begged the question in many places, then he would certainly have been the greatest thinker who had ever lived. As it is, he is merely comic."[90] In like vein, Derrida argued that irreducible events like the incarnation need only be considered as possibilities without insisting on their historical facticity.[91] Perhaps this is what he might have allowed for in terms of a Kierkegaardian thought experiment, namely, that the biblical Jesus could indeed be *thought of,* no more and no less, rather than believed as the Messiah for whom deconstruction had been waiting. Did Derrida at all imagine such a possibility? Arguably, there is no question that deconstruction recognizes in the new norms, values, and practices foundational to the kingdom of heaven described by Jesus in the Sermon on the Mount—say, forgiveness that is indefinite—as part of the common ground to which deconstruction itself aspires. As Caputo has allowed:

> For a Derridean theology, it would seem that the God of gifts, the gift of God, and the gift of God in Jesus are to be thought not in terms of insolvent debt but in terms of giving without debt and in forgiving what debts accumulate . . . Debts are for forgiving, not accumulating. According to the New Testament, the only calculation forgiving allows is that one should forgive seven times a day, and seventy times seven, that is to say, innumerably, countlessly, incalculably. That would seem to be, from Derrida's point of view, the real *Geniestreich* of Jesus.[92]

That said, Holy Writ itself offers us no reason to consign Christ to the intellectual confines of a thought experiment. Returning to Victor Taylor's comparison between the different laughs emitted by Sarah (in Gen 18:12) and by Derrida, what we could perhaps say of Derrida's evident inability to bear witness and to stop his sad laughter, as Taylor put it, is due in no small part to Derrida's urging for a "de-Christification of experience"[93]—for the reasons highlighted in the previous chapter, namely, Derrida's discomfort

---

Rather, his aim was to demonstrate that Levinas should not have been so hasty to dismiss Kierkegaard but could have recovered his interpretation of Abraham for purposes that Derrida and Levinas both shared. Hanson, "Returning (to) The Gift of Death," 1.

90. Kierkegaard, *Søren Kierkegaard's Journals*, 87.
91. Derrida, *Gift of Death*, 49.
92. Caputo, "Apostles of the Impossible," 214–15.
93. Derrida, *Specters of Marx*, 59.

with what he judged as the invisibility, inaccessibility, and irresponsibility of Christ. Despite his insistence that he was awaiting the coming of the messianic, Derrida's apparent decision to remain in his indefinite aporetic moment renders deconstruction a bridge that potentially leads nowhere. In the chorus of the song "Heaven" by the American rock band Talking Heads, heaven is described as a place where nothing ever happens. According to Nicholas Royle, those lyrics provide an apt description of just what the kind of destination envisaged by deconstruction might look like, if one existed at all.[94] But as one might expect from the prophet of aporia, deferral, and undecidability, the highway of deconstruction comes with forks and crossroads—or, perhaps more apposite to deconstruction, a roundabout where travelers continuously loop and settle into a holding pattern of indeterminate duration, even as decisions big and small continue to be rendered amid undecidability. In the final interview he gave before his death in October 2004, Derrida offered this intriguing thought consistent with his other pronouncements on undecidability:

> I don't want to renounce anything, indeed I cannot. Because, you know, learning to live is always *narcissistic* (a concept, let me just note in passing, that I've tried to complicate elsewhere): one wants to live as much as possible, to save oneself, to persevere, and to cultivate all these things which, though infinitely greater and more powerful than oneself, nonetheless form a part of this little "me" that they exceed on all sides. To ask me to renounce what formed me, what I've loved so much, what has been my law, is to ask me to die.[95]

Derrida's disciplined and unequivocal commitment to undecidability—to quote Nietzsche, "a long obedience in the same direction . . . [that] has made life worth living"[96]—is indeed admirable. On the other hand, it implies a persistent privileging of the self despite deconstruction's emphasis on otherness, for what is the presumption of one's prerogative of choice but the height of hubristic autonomy? We recall that Derrida's namesake, the prophet Elijah—the young Jackie was given the middle name Élie (the French equivalent of Elijah or Elias) at his circumcision—remonstrated with the people of Israel at his showdown with the prophets of Baal atop Mount Carmel: "'How long will you waver between two opinions? If the LORD is

---

94. Royle, "Jacques Derrida, Also, Enters into Heaven," 113.
95. Derrida, *Learning to Live Finally*, 29–30, italics original.
96. Nietzsche, *Beyond Good and Evil*, 45.

God, follow him; but if Baal is God, follow him' . . . [but] the people said nothing" (1 Kgs 18:21). But as we have seen, unlike the people before Elijah, deconstruction, led by its prophet, prince, and high priest Élie (Derrida), did not just say nothing in response. Nor would its preference to postpone the coming of Messiah imply that deconstruction would welcome proof of God's existence by fire (1 Kgs 18:24). Derrida's masterful reflection on decision amid undecidability suggests a propensity to wanting the cake and eating it too. In fairness to Derrida, recall (as highlighted above) his confessions about his struggles over indecision that resemble Paul's internal conflict laid bare in Rom 7, although one gets the sense that Derrida remained at his Peniel to the very end, endlessly wrestling and, unlike Jacob, never quite making it across the Jabbok river (Gen 32:22–31).[97] Whether his express refusal to renounce anything includes extending hospitality toward and accommodation of Christ is surely questionable in view of his persistent suspicion against Christology. Deconstruction might have opened the door to the crucified and resurrected Christ, but—by way of Derrida's prodigious scholarship and commentary, by way of deconstruction's insistence that the Messiah for which it awaits is ultimately unknowable and, for that matter, unlikely to show—it does not appear that deconstruction's greatest hero ever entered. And yet, such a refusal of Christ, if indeed that is what it is, cannot be ultimately sustained were deconstruction to hold true to its own logics. After all, how could deconstruction stand in perdurable judgment against all existing messianic and eschatological claims, including and especially the biblical one, when it offers its own rival claim about the messianic, when it harbors its own debts—acknowledged for the most part, but at times conveniently left unsaid—to a Christian eschatology? We will return to this issue in the next chapter.

Deconstruction's Own Private Idaho?

If nothing and nowhere and constitutes a destination, to what and where, then, might deconstruction's endless wait for its impossible God lead? Where might nowhere, where nothing happens, be? Not the *tout autre* or wholly other, I suggest, but the self; or, put another way, the vacuum

---

97. Caputo suggests as much: "Derrida is wrestling with his angel through the night and does not know if, when morning comes, he will find himself in the arms of an angel of the Lord, or the Lord himself, or what! . . . He has faith in faith, and hope in hope, but he has no guarantees." Caputo, "What Do I Love When I Love My God?" 311.

and void of deconstruction's wholly other could only be filled by the self.[98] Despite the overwhelming significance of otherness for deconstruction, Derrida seemed to offer the intriguing suggestion that one's ultimate responsibility is to oneself—a sort of private aestheticism and asceticism, as it were.[99] As he once wrote, "My first and last responsibility, my first and last desire, is that responsibility of responsibility that relates me to what no one else can do in my place . . . we are given over to absolute solitude. No one can speak with us and no one can speak for us; we must take it upon ourselves, each of us must take it upon himself . . ."[100] In another place he offered a similar thought: "It is ethics itself: to learn to live—alone, from oneself, by oneself. Life does not know how to live otherwise. And does one ever do anything else but learn to live, alone, from oneself, by oneself?"[101] And once more from Derrida: "I have been given this image . . . And I have to face some responsibility, political and ethical. It is as if I am indebted to—I don't know to whom—to thinking rigorously, to thinking responsibly. I am in a situation of trying to learn to whom, finally, I am responsible. To discover . . . who is hidden, who gives me orders. It is as if I have a destiny which I have to interpret and decipher."[102]

But how can one, how does one, under those impossible conditions set by deconstruction, discover about or receive direction concerning one's destiny, let alone interpret and decipher those orders, from a God that has already been ruled incomprehensible—not only because we lack the capacity, innate or received, to comprehend God but because a faceless and nameless God remains invisible and inaccessible to us—by deconstruction? Given to an absolute solitude, deconstruction's wait for Messiah is a lonely quest where there can be no possibility of revelation—or, for that matter, reflection[103]—where ethics is reduced to living alone, from and by oneself.

---

98. One here is reminded of Pascal's logic of a "God-shaped vacuum" in human hearts that cannot be filled by created things but only by God made known through Christ.

99. Goldman, "Christian Mystery and Responsibility Gnosticism," 9.

100. Derrida, *Gift of Death*, 44, 57.

101. Derrida, *Specters of Marx*, xvii.

102. Cited in Smith, "Philosopher Gamely In Defense Of His Ideas."

103. As Derrida mused, "How can another see into me, into my most secret self, without my being able to see in there myself and without my being able to see him in me? And if my secret self, that which can be revealed only to the other, to the wholly other, to God if you wish, is a secret that I will never reflect on, that I will never know or experience or possess as my own, then what sense is there in saying that it is 'my' secret, or in saying more generally that a secret *belongs,* that it is proper to or belongs to some

Contra the perceived lack of responsibility of which it accuses Christianity, deconstruction's responsibility is to no one and to nothing but to oneself. After all, any prospect for the immanence and imminence of the *tout autre* is resisted by Derrida's insistence on maintaining distance from the divine, much like how the Israelites kept their distance from the mountain of God for fear of death (Exod 20:18–19). Note the distinct boundary drawn by Derrida, a red line never to be crossed: "To surrender to the other, and this is the impossible, would amount to giving oneself over in going toward the other, to coming toward the other *but without crossing the threshold*, and to respecting, to loving even the invisibility that keeps the other inaccessible."[104] Here, any divine invitation to draw near(er) to God is effectively rebuffed and refused by deconstruction in the name of respecting, loving, and ultimately preserving the purported invisibility and inaccessibility of God. There can be no crossover to the other side, to the side of deconstruction's wholly other. Indeed, the focus remains on the self and what one makes—what one fashions and refashions—of one's impossible God based purely on one's own making, since the possibility that God may desire to communicate and commune with us has already been resisted and refused by the terms of deconstruction.

Why this enduring obsession against crossing the threshold over to the wholly other? Returning to Derrida's debate with Jean-Luc Marion over the latter's insistence that praise of God does not involve predication and the metaphysical assignation of meaning to God's name—for Marion, "Hallelujah! Praise the Lord! God is good!" are pragmatic declarations of pure praise and pure prayer, not predication[105]—Derrida by contrast argued that praise is always directed or targeted at someone or something; in short, the hymn always has something to do with the apophantic (i.e., a predication or categorical statement).[106] Rather than risk sliding into idola-

---

'one,' or to some *other* who remains *someone*? It is perhaps there that we find the secret of secrecy, namely, that it is not a matter of knowing and that it is there for no-one . . . The question of the self: 'who am I?' not in the sense of 'who am I' but 'who is this "I"' that can say 'who'? What is the 'I,' and what becomes of responsibility once the identity of the 'I' trembles *in secret*?" Derrida, *Specters of Marx*, 92, italics original.

104. Derrida, *On the Name*, 74, italics mine.

105. Marion, "In His Name," 28–30.

106. Caputo, "Apostles of the Impossible," 190. Indeed, it was precisely on similar grounds that Derrida criticized Levinas's notion of the wholly other (*tout autre*) because, far as Derrida was concerned, the other for Levinas was quite precisely God and/or other people, rather than an animal or a rock. In other words, the logic of predication was operative in Levinas's philosophy as he had a rather clear and definite idea of what or who

try, deconstruction would instead keep its distance from the divine and protect the gap between sense and reference. No real praise of the wholly other would be possible if we are unable to comprehend it because anything of which we have an adequate comprehension would automatically disqualify it as the wholly other. However, could Derrida be so sure that deconstruction's own quest for the Messiah to whom/which it can finally declare "*oui, oui!*"—a shout of praise, no less!—would not result in the very same hyper-essentialism of which it accuses all the orthodox faiths? In fairness to Derrida, it is worth noting that time and again, the holiness of God precluded his worshipers from becoming too familiar with him. According to Richard Kearney, human responsibility in the relationship between God and man, as defined by the encounter between God and Moses in Exod 3, consists in a dual injunction to humankind neither to become overly distant nor overly familiar with God: "Moses, remember, is summoned to approach but also to remove his sandals and keep his distance. A safe distance, a sacred reserve"—a twofold summons that beckons, "Come!" and at the same time warns, "but not too near!"[107] And yet have we not also been enjoined to "enter the Most Holy Place by the blood of Jesus" (Heb 10:19)? For Christians, the atonement of Christ for their sin has rendered it possible for that chasm between sinful humankind and a holy God to be crossed, by way of our belief in God and in the name of Jesus and his redemptive work. But absent Christology—absent the way, the door, and the bridge by which the wholly other of the Bible could be accessed (John 14:6)—it is hard to see how deconstruction could have ever imagined the possibility that the threshold that held Derrida back could in fact be traversed—not because humankind stormed the place of the wholly other by sheer force but that Christ, by his sacrifice at Calvary, had torn the veil separating "the Holy of Holies," the earthly dwelling place of God's presence, from the rest of the temple where humankind dwelt (Heb 9). This is a core issue to which we shall return in the following chapter.

Indeed, what deconstruction awaits could ultimately be the self, where self relates to itself in secret, *where the self is none other than God*. As Derrida averred:

> God is the name of the possibility I have of keeping a secret that is visible from the interior but not from the exterior. Once such a structure of conscience exists, of being-with-oneself, of speaking,

---

his wholly other was. Derrida, "Violence and Metaphysics."

107. Kearney, "God Who May Be," 160.

that is, of producing invisible sense, once I have within me, *thanks to the invisible word as such,* a witness that others cannot see, and who is therefore *at the same time other than me and more intimate with me than myself,* once I can have a secret relationship with myself and not tell everything, once there is secrecy and secret witnessing within me, then what I call God exists, (there is) what I call God in me, (it happens that) I call myself God—a phrase that is difficult to distinguish from "God calls me," for it is on that condition that I can call myself or that I am called in secret. God is in me, he is the absolute "me" or "self," he is that structure of invisible interiority that is called, in Kierkegaard's sense, subjectivity.[108]

With the prospect of divine immanence and imminence already elided in deconstruction's rigorous insistence on spiritual and social distance vis-à-vis its wholly other, it is perhaps not surprising that in the echo chamber of selfness, the inevitable conclusion and only recourse available is Derrida's apparent claim above to self-divinity: *I call myself God.* Is this where Derrida pushed so hard on the logic of interiorization—the "structure of invisible interiority" as he called it,[109] where God and he became essentially interchangeable—that he ended up with the totalization, idolization, and deification of self? Does not the impossible, invisible, and inaccessible God of deconstruction pave the way toward a potential invasion and colonization of other, including the wholly other, by the self—where, per Derrida's formulation, "God calls me" becomes virtually indistinguishable from "I call myself God"—within the hermetically sealed confines of their secret interiorized relationship about which no one knows? Indeed, to what and where else might deconstruction inexorably lure and lead one but back to oneself and the worship of self? In a marathon address that reportedly lasted ten hours which Derrida gave at the 1997 Cérisy conference in his honor, he made a claim that was astonishing even by his standards: "I am like a child ready for the apocalypse, I am the apocalypse itself, that is to say, the ultimate and first event of the end, the unveiling and the verdict."[110]

---

108. Derrida, *Gift of Death*, 108–09, italics original.

109. In his exchange with Kevin Hart, Derrida explained that when speaking of the infinite distance of God, he was not referring to distance as conventionally understood but, rather, to alterity: "When Levinas speaks of infinite distance, he means that God is absolutely other. It is not about distance, of course. So there is no contradiction between what you [Hart] said about the God close to myself, or even more interior to myself than myself, and God's infinite distance. It is the same." Derrida in Hart, "Absolute Interruption," 201.

110. Derrida, *Animal that Therefore I Am*, 12.

Awaiting Deconstruction's Impossible God

As Jean-Luc Nancy, who helped convene one of the first Cérisy conferences dedicated to Derrida, once observed about his friend, "He who contributed so much to deconstructing 'presence' was overwhelmingly present."[111] In the end, the wholly other faded, and only Derrida seemed to remain. But in good deconstructive fashion, we should add "perhaps."

---

111. Cited in Peeters, *Derrida*, 420.

4

Hello from the Other Side

The God of the Impossible Speaks

Then the Lord spoke to Job out of the storm (Job 38:1).

The Lord said, "Go out and stand on the mountain in the presence of the Lord, for the Lord is about to pass by." Then a great and powerful wind tore the mountains apart and shattered the rocks before the Lord, but the Lord was not in the wind. After the wind there was an earthquake, but the Lord was not in the earthquake. After the earthquake came a fire, but the Lord was not in the fire. And after the fire came a gentle whisper (1 Kgs 19:11–12).

A MINOR SCENE FROM the 1989 movie, *Dead Poets Society*, has long stayed with me: the teacher John Keating (played by the late Robin Williams with uncharacteristic restraint) pretends not to hear the overtures of his student until he is greeted with the opening line from Whitman's poem, "O Captain! My Captain!" In his comparative assessment of the questions to or about God posed by three very different men—Job of Old Testament renown, Augustine the bishop of Hippo Regius, and Derrida the religious atheist—Graham Ward, as noted in the preceding chapter, suggested that the questions posed by Job in his struggle with theodicy, and those by Augustine in the account of his path to redemption and faith in *The Confessions*, can neither be understood nor be even conceivable were it not for the relations of those respective speakers/writers to their God.[1] In his quest for reprieve

---

1. Ward, "Questioning God."

and vindication, Job never once let go of his belief that his Redeemer lives and that he (Job) would see God (Job 19:25–27). Indeed, the fact that when God (finally) spoke to Job out of the storm (in Job 38:1–3)—and doing so in a way quite unexpected and even terrifying—the fact remains that God communicated in response to Job's protracted torturous wait for a divine rejoinder to his abject circumstances. In probing his own desires—"What do I love when I love my God," the question that so inspired Derrida's own ruminations—Augustine left no doubt regarding his core belief; as the opening salvo of *The Confessions* declares, "Great are You, O Lord, and greatly to be praised; great is Your power, and Your wisdom infinite." For Ward, those respective claims reflect relationships both Job and Augustine had with God that suggest their intimate knowledge of him. God can be known; indeed, he desires to be known and acknowledged by his creation. "God neither could have been, nor ought to have been, unknown," as Tertullian, the early Christian author and apologist from Carthage, insisted. "Could not have been, because of His greatness; ought not to have been, because of His goodness . . ."[2]

Evidently, the God of the Bible who reveals and avails of himself to us is not deconstruction's wholly other of whom or which nothing can or should be known. As we have seen, it is not just the opposition of apophatic/negative theology to the assumption that the *mysterium tremendum* could at all be grasped by the human mind that troubled Derrida—think, for instance, of Spinoza's contention that intuitive knowledge about God, nature, and the universe is theoretically possible—but equally the perceptibly hyperessentialist end of all theology to protect and preserve the eminence of God, and the potential ramifications for idolatry and injustice brought about by such a move. As Derrida saw it, the work of deconstruction is to demythologize by dismantling manmade idols of all kinds, including the orthodox religions, and to pave the way to the coming of an impossible justice—a justice hitherto denied by concrete messianisms that have historically facilitated war not peace—because deconstruction itself is justice. But if neither knowing and naming God, nor the possibility for any revelation concerning the messianic anticipated by deconstruction—a messianic endlessly deferred, in any event—were permissible, then what can be said in response to deconstruction's questions about God?[3] Indeed, could a

---

2. Tertullian, *Writings of Tertullian*, 65.

3. "To whom, then, are Derrida's questions addressed? Who receives them?" as Graham Ward wandered aloud. "The play in his book *The Post Card: From Socrates to Freud*

God who is wholly other even be God at all, since there could be nothing at all that we could hope to know about such a God? Be that as it may, it needs to be said—and here I share the views of careful readers of Derrida like John Caputo and Ward himself—that deconstruction, in both text and tone, is neither atheistic nor nihilistic in orientation, but rather *agnostic*, marked by an "interminable openness" to an indeterminate Other.[4] Yet it seems that, unlike Job and Augustine, no overture directed to God ever stemmed from Derrida and deconstruction for that would constitute, by their estimation, an act in predication.

This chapter aims to furnish a Christian rejoinder to the questions and objections that arise from deconstruction's religion without religion, as discussed in the preceding chapters. Notwithstanding its professed openness, deconstruction's apparent resistance to welcome the biblical Jesus has not in any way lessen the fundamental significance of deconstruction's contributions—not just in bringing the religious and the messianic back into mainstream philosophical discourse but, as the proverbial voice in the wilderness, in speaking prophetically to Christianity's longstanding proclivity to entertain idolatries both in heart and head and to engage in injustices by its own hand. Tragically, Israel—and the church—have had a sordid history of murdering its prophets between the temple and the altar and crucifying them outside the city walls. There is ample evidence, as seen in the previous chapters, that deconstruction arguably shares common cause with Yahweh's prophets—indeed, with Christ himself[5]—against idolatry and injustice. And yet, for the reasons discussed earlier, it stops short at saying yes to the crucified Christ as Messiah, whom deconstruction seems to view as both a stumbling block and foolishness (1 Cor 1:23).

Who's Knocking on Whose Door?

Deconstruction's quest for the Messiah suggests a readiness, as Bob Dylan once put it, to knock on the door to heaven. But it is a knocking that, by the logics and assumptions of deconstruction, anticipates no plausible response,

---

and Beyond would suggest that [his] questions . . . are unanswerable. But then what are the implications of unanswerability? It is not the questioning of one consciously committed to God. And I would greatly hesitate to suggest unconscious or anonymous commitment." Ward, "Questioning God," 277.

4. Ward, *Barth, Derrida and the Language of Theology*, 220.
5. Caputo, *What Would Jesus Deconstruct?*

neither from the God of the Bible nor any other deity venerated by a concrete messianism. Indeed, as we have seen, deconstruction's quest is not even in response to any discernable overture from above. According to the biblical narrative, the divine invitation to seek, ask, and knock—coupled with the promise and assurance of divine response—has been and continues to be issued. And if John Keating in *Dead Poets Society* enjoined his students to "seize the day" (*carpe diem*) in response to the moment, so too does Holy Writ in response to the divine invitation: "Today, if only you would hear his voice . . ." (Ps 95:7b).[6] The following expressions of invitation, taken from both the Old and New Testaments, are by no means exhaustive, but they furnish a sense of the unambiguous summons by the biblical Other which deconstruction deems impossible from its wholly other:

> But if from there you seek the LORD your God, you will find him if you seek him with all your heart and with all your soul (Deut 4:29).
>
> I love those who love me, and those who seek me find me (Prov 8:17).
>
> I have not spoken in secret, from somewhere in a land of darkness; I have not said to Jacob's descendants, "Seek me in vain." I, the LORD, speak the truth; I declare what is right (Isa 45:19).
>
> This is what the LORD says, he who made the earth, the LORD who formed it and established it—the LORD is his name: "Call to me and I will answer you and tell you great and unsearchable things you do not know" (Jer 33:2–3).
>
> Ask and it will be given to you; seek and you will find; knock and the door will be opened to you. For everyone who asks receives; the one who seeks finds; and to the one who knocks, the door will be opened (Matt 7:7).
>
> On the last and greatest day of the festival, Jesus stood and said in a loud voice, "Let anyone who is thirsty come to me and drink. Whoever believes in me, as Scripture has said, rivers of living water will flow from within them" (John 7:37–38).

---

6. However, in contrast to deconstruction's presumption of an endless wait, the psalmist's "today" has a shelf life; as David wrote in another psalm, "Therefore let all the faithful pray to you *while you may be found* . . ." (Ps 32:6a, italics mine).

> The Spirit and the bride say, "Come!" And let the one who hears say, "Come!" Let the one who is thirsty come; and let the one who wishes take the free gift of the water of life (Rev 22:17).

Come, call, ask, seek, knock. The divine invitation is not just for prospective God-seekers to go toward God, but it is equally the invitation to open the door to welcome God, he who has taken the initiative to come toward us, right to our very doorstep: "Here I am! I stand at the door and knock. If anyone hears my voice and opens the door, I will come in and eat with that person, and they with me" (Rev 3:20).[7] Despite its professed wait for Messiah, deconstruction is tone deaf to any of the above expressions of the divine invitation. Indeed, none of those possibilities could even be conceivable—no calling to God, no asking of or seeking him or knocking on his door, nor opening of the door to the divine visitor—because, as we have seen, deconstruction rejects the notion that the God which it awaits is knowable, whether through humankind's efforts to apprehend and comprehend the divine, or, for that matter, divine revelation since the logic of deconstruction is precisely to embargo revelation.[8] All there is left, it seems, is to lament alongside Estragon in *Waiting for Godot*: "Nothing happens, nobody comes, nobody goes, it's awful!" And from all that Derrida said and wrote concerning his endless prayers, tears, and sighs,[9] his waiting for a "death" he fought so hard to postpone had probably been just as awful and tragic for him as the next person. As Victor Taylor observed, Derrida the jocular saint draws us toward laughter and binds us to nothing because of his inability to bear witness or to stop his sad laughter because deconstruction knows not what it awaits.[10] And yet the God of the Bible is he who—according to a 2007 survey of Muslims who converted to become

---

7. Granted, there is controversy surrounding the purported "misuse" of this verse by evangelists—an example might be Francis Chan's *Crazy Love*, which is entirely centered around Rev 3:20—because the words of Christ here are more properly addressed to believers (the church at Laodicea) rather than nonbelievers. Chan with Yankoski, *Crazy Love*. But even as Martin Luther once wrote regarding that verse and its applicability to "the ungodly," fraught with evangelistic implications: "The righteous always act [in fear] as if the Lord saw them. But the ungodly walk along smugly, as if God had His eyelids closed and did not see them, even though He examines them, too, and knocks, warning their conscience, as Rev 3:20 says: 'I stand at the door and knock, etc.'" Luther, *Luther's Works*.

8. Labarthe, *Typography*, 118.

9. Caputo, *Prayers and Tears of Jacques Derrida*.

10. Taylor, "Divisible Derridas," 3.

Christ-followers[11]—makes himself known, unsolicited, to the most unexpected audiences through not just his written word, but also dreams and revelations that affirm that word. Speaking through the prophet Isaiah, God furnished this astonishing statement: "I revealed myself to those who did not ask for me; I was found by those who did not seek me. To a nation that did not call on my name, I said, 'Here am I, here am I'" (Isa 65:1). This is not the impossible God of deconstruction from whom no revelation is conceivable let alone anticipated, but the God of the impossible of the Bible who invites, informs, instructs, and even inveighs. There are at least three places in Scripture where God, the LORD, let it be known that there is nothing too hard or impossible for him: "I am the LORD, the God of all mankind. Is anything too hard for me?" (Jer 32:27); "Jesus looked at them and said, 'With man this is impossible, but with God all things are possible'" (Matt 19:26); and again, "Jesus looked at them and said, 'With man this is impossible, but not with God; all things are possible with God'" (Mark 10:27).

It is tempting to ponder, with the memory of that scene recounted earlier from *Dead Poets Society*, whether God might have turned a deaf ear to (or, more probably, is not permitted to address) deconstruction's questions given the apparent lack of the requisite overture from the inquirer. But recall that this is precisely the express burden and yoke—his *cross*, as Derrida put it[12]—which deconstruction feels impelled to bear indefinitely. Indeed, in riposte to Kevin Hart's suggestion that aporia and undecidability were a gift, Derrida declared that he could not accept the notion of such as a gift, which for him spelled reconciliation or resolution or the possibility for such—akin, perhaps, to theodicy's effort to vindicate divine goodness and providence in view of the existence of evil—so committed was he (Derrida) to living and suffering in undecidability. As Derrida explained to Hart:

> As soon as I interpret the aporia in which I suffer as a gift, if I really experience the aporia—the aporia is not simply just a theme or a formalized logic but simply the tragedy of my life—as a gift, if I am sure that aporia has been given to me by God, then that is the end; that is a reconciliation. To experience the aporia I will never know if it is being given to me as a gift or if it has been given to me as

---

11. Woodberry, Shubin, and Marks, "Why Muslims Follow Jesus."
12. Kearney, "On the Gift," 73.

death or a blow or as a punishment or torture. If you are sure that aporia was given as a gift, I envy you.[13]

The impression fostered here of a person bearing a yoke he was probably not meant to bear, but nonetheless felt compelled to do so, is unmistakable. Perhaps, not unlike how a fellow North African, Simon of Cyrene, was unexpectedly press-ganged by Roman legionnaires into carrying the cross for Jesus on the Via Dolorosa (Luke 23:26), Derrida and deconstruction found themselves in a similar predicament, less for Jesus of Nazareth than the inscrutable Messiah for which deconstruction waits without waiting. But if deconstruction, as Caputo has urged, could be understood as in the service of the gospel, could it not therefore be said that Derrida—father not of Alexander and Rufus (Mark 15:21), but of Pierre and Jean (and Daniel)—was a modern-day Simon who served his Godless God at his/her/its time of need, by bearing his/her/its cross? Perhaps, like Simon, Derrida did not choose the cross he bore, nor did he pick the time of its bearing. "We don't always choose the moment of our suffering," as John Piper once mused in his reflection on the role Simon of Cyrene played in the passion narrative. "They come upon us in unexpected ways, frightening ways, heavy ways, painful ways, seemingly random ways."[14] In a sense, the same could be said of the burdens of aporia and undecidability—equally unexpected, frightening, heavy, painful, and seemingly random—that come upon deconstruction and which it feels compelled to endlessly bear. But when we consider the likelihood that deconstruction has eschewed the divine invitation—and coupled with, as we saw earlier, deconstruction's suspicions with Christology—the notion that Derrida might have entertained and even accepted the following summons by the Son of God becomes highly questionable:

> At that time Jesus said, 'I praise you, Father, Lord of heaven and earth, because you have hidden these things from the wise and learned, and revealed them to little children. Yes, Father, for this is what you were pleased to do. All things have been committed to me by my Father. No one knows the Son except the Father, and no one knows the Father except the Son and those to whom the Son chooses to reveal him," as Jesus declared. "Come to me, all you who are weary and burdened, and I will give you rest. Take my yoke upon you and learn from me, for I am gentle and humble in

---

13. Hart, "Absolute Interruption," 201–02.
14. Piper, "What's the Significance of Simon Carrying Jesus's Cross?"

heart, and you will find rest for your souls. For my yoke is easy and my burden is light (Matt 28:25–30).

It is interesting to note in the above passage that Jesus, referencing "the wise and the learned," presented worldly wisdom as an unwarranted burden that brings weariness to its bearers—an unbearable load for which he (Jesus) offers his in exchange. One wonders whether any such an exchange of yokes, burdens, and crosses—exchanging deconstruction's impossible load for the light and easy load promised by Christ—ever took place for Derrida. If it were easier for a camel to go through the eye of a needle than for a rich man to enter the kingdom of God (Matt 19:24), could it not be said that the treasures and resources held and deployed by deconstruction, essential and integral as they are to dismantling idols and delivering justice, inadvertently obstruct the way to the kingdom of God? "For with much wisdom comes much sorrow," so said the Teacher, "the more knowledge, the more grief" (Eccl 1:18); as we have seen, Derrida's cross-bearing proved to be a journey strewn with endless prayers, tears, and sad laughter, awaiting a messiah who never comes. By now it is clear that deconstruction, at least by Derrida's hand, paves the way toward a kind of openness to the religious and the messianic through an unremitting war against idolatry and injustice. But while it seeks to deliver a yes to life, it effectively stops short of saying yes to life *in Christ*. On the one hand, deconstruction contributes powerfully to the dismantlement of arguments and pretensions that set themselves up against the knowledge of God (2 Cor 10:5a); scholars like Caputo and Andrew Shepherd are surely not incorrect to describe Jesus as a deconstructionist par excellence who, as the proverbial prophetic voice in the wilderness, confronted the religious hypocrisies of his day and pointed the way—indeed, declaring himself to be the only way to the heavenly Father (John 14:6)—to freedom in God.[15] On the other hand, deconstruction does its dismantling work *without* taking captive thoughts and subjecting them in obedience to Christ (2 Cor 10:5b).

What prospects are there for completing deconstruction's unfinished bridge to the gospel? Are there available resources within deconstruction that, not unlike tree stumps that look dead but from which life can and will spring forth, provide a way to Christ? Short of the obvious answer—that deconstruction ought to suspend its suspicion toward concrete messianisms—and by staying true to its express openness to the messianic, including the prospect of the biblical Jesus as the Messiah for whom deconstruction

---

15. Caputo, *What Would Jesus Deconstruct?* and Shepherd, *Gift of the Other*.

awaits, it bears highlighting Derrida's deeply ingrained sensitivity to the other and the unexpected gift that sustained meaningful engagement with the other brings, namely, the favor of an unmerited grace: "[G]race would perhaps come when the writing of the other absolves you, from time to time, from the infinite *double bind* and first of all, such is a gift's condition, absolves itself, unbinds itself from this double bind, unburdens or clears itself, it, the language [*langue*] of writing, this given trace that always comes from the other, even if it is no one."[16] To which the Christian cannot help but respond: yes, but, unlike Derrida's "no one," grace is someone personally knowable and gloriously namable, even Christ Jesus. And yet, deconstruction's indebtedness to Christianity is palpably evident—as Derrida regularly insisted, "a radicalization is always indebted to the very thing it radicalizes"[17]—not least because, as we have seen, Derrida sought so hard to deny any plausibility to the biblical Jesus as the Messiah for which his religion without religion presumably longs. As Caputo has also conceded, deconstruction can rightly be viewed as but one among a host of messianisms that is indebted to and situated within "a determinate historical identity and pedigree."[18] In an unusual admission of deconstruction's "shortcomings"—significant in the light of Derrida's critique in *Specters of Marx* of specific historical political claims as always and already embedded with hints of Christian eschatology—Caputo goes on to say:

> In fact, and short of its own intentions, by distinguishing the messianic from the messianisms, it is recognizably a reinscription of a biblical or messianic religion, of the religions of the Book (rather than of Buddhism or Zoroastrianism). Against its own purpose (and how could it be otherwise?) it does indeed bear specific traces of "Christian proclamation" and "Jewish eschatology" . . . Having begun where it is, deconstruction is identifiable and locatable within the political and biblical traditions of the west, within the Shema at the beginning and the call to "Come" at the end of the New Testament . . .[19]

At least two interrelated implications arise from here. On the one hand, in refusing the historicity and humanity of Christ, Derridean deconstruction risks committing that for which it criticizes others, namely, their

---

16. Derrida, *Derrida and Negative Theology*, 26, italics original.
17. Derrida, *Specters of Marx*, 116.
18. Caputo, "What Do I Love When I Love My God?" 308.
19. Caputo, "What Do I Love When I Love My God?" 308.

neglect of history.[20] Deconstruction is surely not alone in its relentless critique of ahistorical proclivities in self-professed historical narratives; works like Philip Yancey's *The Jesus I Never Knew*, for example, highlight how various Christian traditions, including evangelical Christianity, are themselves guilty of privileging their domesticated caricatures of Christ that bear little resemblance to the biblical Jesus.[21] On the other hand, despite its obvious debt to Christianity—Derrida's *The Gift of Death* is a prime example—deconstruction seems to conveniently forget Christianity as "its other" through erasing traces of the latter—again, doing exactly the very thing it has sought to expose in other intellectual, literary, and cultural traditions. After all, Derrida's religion without religion, his messianicity without messianism, boils down to an attempt to escape—perhaps even to erase and elide—the crucified Christ as embodied in his call to "de-Christify" one's lived experience.[22]

No Other Name

Deconstruction's principal concern over any naming of God has to do with theology's aim to furnish a proper and identifiable God; or, as Caputo once put it, "a proper or identifiable Giver which gives us a proper or identifiable Gift."[23] As we also saw, deconstruction's suspicion over Christology—especially the Bible's claim concerning the singularity and centrality of the life, death, burial, and resurrection of Jesus—centers on the insistence on the exclusivity of Christ for salvation. But what does it really mean to declare the name, Jesus? It is probably fair to say of the various people who interacted with Jesus during his brief stint on earth—Mary and Joseph, the disciples, the Pharisee Nicodemus who visited Jesus by night, the Roman prefect Pontius Pilate who questioned truth and had Jesus crucified at the behest of the crowds, the many people Jesus healed and restored, the Pharisees and religious teachers with whom Jesus debated, the list goes on—that none could claim to have fully grasped Jesus in all his complexity and mystery. Deconstruction is correct to warn of the innumerable unfortunate attempts by many over the past two millennia—and many more will continue to do

---

20. Goldman, "Christian Mystery and Responsibility Gnosticism in Derrida's *The Gift of Death*."
21. Yancey, *Jesus I Never Knew*.
22. Derrida, *Specters of Marx*, 59.
23. Caputo, *Prayers and Tears of Jacques Derrida*, 165.

so in the future—to "nail down" Jesus, figuratively and literally. But much like the way Jesus eluded the crowds seeking either to crown him or to kill him before his time, so also does he continue to elude our efforts, no matter how well intentioned, to fix and frame him to suit our purposes and agendas. In that regard, Caputo is correct to insist that our efforts to name God merely reflect our desire for God, no more and no less.[24]

Arguably, deconstruction's suspicion over theology's participation in idolatry through its determinative naming of God—understood at least in terms of Caputo's "a proper or identifiable Giver which gives us a proper or identifiable Gift"—is in a sense mitigatable, perhaps even reconcilable (although one hesitates to use such language with deconstructionists!) by the fact that what God ultimately reveals to us is his very self: *the indeterminable God gives us his indeterminable self*. As Michael Scanlon has put it succinctly, "The highest gift of God, the gift of God that we call our salvation, is nothing less than God."[25] Here we are reminded that in the gospel of Luke, Jesus invites his disciples to boldly seek and ask of God because if earthly fathers know how to give good gifts to their children, then how much more would the heavenly Father give the Holy Spirit—the very Spirit of God himself, no less—to those who ask him (Luke 11:13). Scanlon cites from Augustine: "One of Augustine's favorite words for the Spirit, the Holy Spirit, is the Spirit of God, the Spirit of Christ, is God's Gift, the *donum Dei*. Augustine puts it very nicely: 'God gives us many gifts, but *Deus est qui Deum dat*' ('God is He Who gives God')."[26] In gifting us his Spirit, God is gifting us his very self; as Paul wrote to the Corinthian believers, "*Now the Lord is the Spirit*, and where the Spirit of the Lord is, there is freedom. And we all, who with unveiled faces contemplate the Lord's glory, are being transformed into his image with ever-increasing glory, *which comes from the Lord, who is the Spirit*" (2 Cor 3:17–18, italics mine). If so, does this necessarily mean that God who gives excessively and generously of himself—all his boundless omnipresence, omniscience, and omnipotence—also, by this very act of self-giving, effectively contains and delimits himself, as deconstruction assumes?

Perhaps more than some Christians, it was, unsurprisingly, Derrida who most appreciated the immensity and profundity of the notion that what God gives the world is his very self; in another place, Scanlon recounts

---

24. Caputo, "What Do I Love When I Love My God?" 300.
25. Scanlon in Kearney, "On the Gift," 54.
26. Scanlon in Kearney, "On the Gift," 54.

how, at an academic conference in 1997, Derrida was visibly moved when someone quoted to him another of Augustine's phrases: *Imo quantus Deus est qui dat Deum* ("Indeed, how much must he who gives God be God").[27] Whether this understanding is sufficient to disrupt and lift deconstruction's indefinite embargo of divine revelation is unclear.[28] If anything, contrary to deconstruction's rejection of the possibility of crossover to its wholly other, the God who gives God, as we have seen, invites us to draw near to him and in turn he will draw near to us (Jas 4:8). Indeed, idolatry and injustice are more likely to arise when one distances herself from God; in Exod 32, the Israelites resorted to making the golden calf not least because they maintained their distance from God. Speaking of the Christian's constant exposure to risk from her vulnerable exposure to God—because her life is in his hands and her soul is laid bare before his penetrating gaze—Kevin Hart contends that it is impossible to subject God successfully to metaphysical capture, try as hard as one might:

> No one can contain God within a horizon of expectation. We remain vulnerable to his surprise. He can interrupt our lives, even though He is closer to us than our own breathing . . . He [is] not infinitely distant from us but infinitely close to us: we can never step back far enough and bring him into focus. If we could step back that far, we would make him into an idol. But we cannot take such a backward step with God.[29]

Or, as Mike Mason has observed, there is a level of spiritual experience that God's children undergo which no amount of theology can ever hope to conceptualize let alone capture fully. In his reflection on the Christian's experience with suffering, Mason writes:

> It is a very strange thing to be a Christian and yet feel alienated from God. Yet in all honesty, is this not a real dimension of every Christian's experience? What is strange is that all our theology tells us just the opposite—that we are His dearly loved children and He will never forsake us. But there is a level of spiritual experience that theology cannot touch. Just as there are black holes in space that no telescope can probe, so there are depths to reality that theology tries to plumb but never can. Our creed may be ever so orthodox, but how shall we fare when God Himself begins doing

---

27. Scanlon, "Deconstruction of Religion," 277.
28. Labarthe, *Typography*, 118.
29. Hart, "Absolute Interruption," 202.

the unorthodox? . . . Oddly enough, if our faith makes no practical allowance for confusion, alienation, and oppression, then Christianity becomes a pollyanna religion in which the very possibility of the Lord's direct and supernatural intervention has been leached away.[30]

Deconstruction's resistance toward what Derrida called concrete messianisms is tied to the perceived idolatries practiced and injustices perpetrated by religionists in the name of this or that deity, including the God of the Bible whether Yahweh or Christ. Crucially, deconstruction understands its resistance in terms of saving and salvaging the name of God, rather than refusing and rejecting God. Offering the sober reminder that the name of God has served as both tinder and fuel for some of humanity's most famous fires from time immemorial—which explains why the name of God can be so very dangerous—Caputo observed that:

> The name of God is very simply the most famous and richest name we have to signify both an open-ended excess and an inaccessible mystery. That is why I insist I do not "reduce" the event to religion when I speak of a theology of the event but on the contrary find a place to safeguard its irreducibility and unconditionality . . . The name of God is one of the names that Derrida has in mind when he meditates upon the phrase *sauf le nom*, "safe the name," an expression that for Derrida means both: let us keep this name safe, let us save it, but also: God is everything save (*sauf*/except) the name, save or except what the name names explicitly, everything except the excess that exceeds what is explicitly named. The name of God names everything save the event that is sheltered by this name, which is an event that solicits and invites, calls and signals us, but is never finally named.[31]

The distinction deconstruction makes between the presumed reductionism that any utterance of the name of God rendered by theology—for that matter, by the confessing community of faith—and deconstruction's solution to never name God and, as such, avoid his/her/its untoward determinative capture, arises from deconstruction's insistence that God is unattainable and any effort to name God amounts to a vain attempt to touch and tame him. "Is not the *tout autre* [wholly other] the shore we never reach, always other than anything we can conceive or see coming?"

---

30. Mason, *Gospel According to Job*, 116.
31. Caputo, "Spectral Hermeneutics," 53–54.

as Caputo has written elsewhere. "But in theology the *tout autre* goes under the determinate name of God, which it is the vocation of theology to save, whereas deconstruction says no more than *tout autre*. But in theology itself, for Derrida, God is truly God, is beyond God and *Gottheit*, only if God 'slips away' (*dérober*) from the grasp of knowledge."[32] And just to be sure, Caputo in yet another place doubles down on this argument. In his appropriation of Gilles Deleuze's concept of the event, Caputo argues that no act of naming can fully apprehend and capture the event it names: "The name of God is the name of an event that is greater than anything that exists. If anything does exist, that is not what is named by the name of God, or, rather, it is not the event that is harbored or contained within the name of God."[33] In other words, to claim that something exists would be to exhaust the event because any event that has already been named in or under the name of God is thereby not allowed to assume its final or highest form. Instead, the evolution or transformation of the event has been violently arrested and attenuated and its very becoming is effectively precluded from realization. (What is even more intriguing is Caputo's criticism against Deleuze for failing to anticipate that the kingdom of God described in the New Testament could properly constitute an event that continues to elude the vainglorious attempts by Christians to name and capture it in the here and now.[34] Known for his suspicions against theodicy as Christian self-defensiveness in the face of human violence and suffering, Deleuze arguably rejected the Christian perspective that Christ suffered once and for all and thereby serves as the analogical basis for the inherent meaning and promise of all suffering.[35]) And as suggested in the previous chapter, deconstruction's purported openness to the messianic stops short, for all intents and purposes, at the kingdom of God—notwithstanding Caputo's evident receptiveness to that possibility—because of its agnosticism toward Christ.

This is not to imply that deconstructionists believe that no naming is ever conceivable or desirable. But what they want to be clear about, and correctly so, is that the act of naming does not effectively nail down the entity in question—to determine, once and for all, the very presence of the

---

32. Caputo, "Apostles of the Impossible," 193.
33. Caputo, "Spectral Hermeneutics," 56.
34. Caputo, "Spectral Hermeneutics," 60.
35. Barber, *Deleuze and the Naming of God*. Interestingly, despite Derrida's known reservations against Christology, nowhere does Caputo criticize Derrida the way he does Deleuze.

entity—but, at best, it merely reflects that for which we hope and wish. "The name of God is not God but the name of our desire for God, the name that points us to God," as Caputo has put it. "The other promised to us in and by language always remains out-standing, still to come, still promised, structurally, for as long as we are speaking, rather like a Messiah who does not show up. To speak is to succumb to messianic longing, or rather to embrace and affirm it."[36] For Derrida, the determinate historical figure of Jesus, like the figures in other world religions, are but one among many determinations of a faith that remains determinable in other ways, that can take different forms in different times and different places, where their names may be completely unknown—even as those figures harbor within themselves a future that has yet to unfold. In other words, what deconstruction insists on is the *contingent* and *transmutable* quality of those figures as well as the names with which they are associated. At the very least, they insist on the indeterminate and uncertain nature of things. Again, in Caputo's words:

> [T]he best thing we can say of God is not that God is the act of all acts, but that God is the possibility of all possibilities, the possibility of the impossible, the highest possible "perhaps." The name of God is one of our best names, and Derrida loves it very much and wants to save it. But however inescapable it is for us, here and now, it is not definitive or indispensable, and it may be in time to come the name of God, and maybe even the name of love, will give way and that it will do so precisely in the name of what we now call love and now call God. Maybe. Perhaps. We do not know.[37]

The caveat that Derrida, Caputo, and deconstruction collectively raise above against any determinate naming is a very important concern to which we shall return in a moment. At this juncture, it is worthwhile to recall what the Scriptures say about the name of Jesus, not least from Peter first and then Paul, the two men designated as the apostles to the Jews and the Gentiles, respectively[38]:

---

36. Caputo, "What Do I Love When I Love My God?" 300.
37. Caputo, "What Do I Love When I Love My God?" 311–12.
38. Positing Derrida and Jean-Luc Marion as two "apostles of the impossible," Caputo once contended that "Derrida is a more Pauline figure, who wants all the *gentiles*, the *goyim*, to share in the good news, while Marion is more Petrine and insistent on a straiter gate." Caputo, "Apostles of the Impossible," 187. Yet Paul's unequivocal emphasis on Jesus as Lord and Savior, in the Rom 10 passage below and numerous other places in his epistles, is clearly a point of contention for deconstruction. Moreover, in dismissing Marion as more Petrine, Caputo did not account for Peter's conversion of Cornelius the Roman

> Then Peter, filled with the Holy Spirit, said to them: "Rulers and elders of the people! If we are being called to account today for an act of kindness shown to a man who was lame and are being asked how he was healed, then know this, you and all the people of Israel: *It is by the name of Jesus Christ of Nazareth*, whom you crucified but whom God raised from the dead, that this man stands before you healed. Jesus is "the stone you builders rejected, which has become the cornerstone." *Salvation is found in no one else, for there is no other name under heaven given to mankind by which we must be saved* (Acts 4:8–12, italics mine).
>
> If you declare with your mouth, *"Jesus is Lord,"* and believe in your heart that God raised him from the dead, you will be saved. For it is with your heart that you believe and are justified, and it is with your mouth that you profess your faith and are saved. As Scripture says, "Anyone who believes in him will never be put to shame." For there is no difference between Jew and Gentile—the same Lord is Lord of all and richly blesses all who call on him, for, *"Everyone who calls on the name of the Lord will be saved"* (Rom 10:9–13, italics mine).

Of the one who declared of himself as "the way and the truth and the life" and as the only conduit through whom all are to go through if they wish to access the heavenly Father (John 14:6), the (unnamed) writer of Hebrews had this to say about Jesus:

> Therefore, brothers and sisters, since we have confidence to enter the Most Holy Place by the blood of Jesus, by a new and living way opened for us through the curtain, that is, his body, and since we have a great priest over the house of God, let us draw near to God with a sincere heart and with the full assurance that faith brings, having our hearts sprinkled to cleanse us from a guilty conscience and having our bodies washed with pure water. Let us hold unswervingly to the hope we profess, for he who promised is faithful (Heb 10:19–23).

And if secondhand testimonies are not enough, the following words reportedly uttered by Jesus—granted, conveyed through an intermediary, the apostle John—identifies himself unequivocally as the returning Messiah:

---

centurion and his family, which occurred after Peter's vision concerning the consumption of animals deemed unclean under Jewish dietary laws, which Peter subsequently interpreted as the extension of God's salvation to the Gentiles (Acts 10 and 11:1–18).

> Look, I am coming soon! My reward is with me, and I will give to each person according to what they have done. I am the Alpha and the Omega, the First and the Last, the Beginning and the End. Blessed are those who wash their robes, that they may have the right to the tree of life and may go through the gates into the city. Outside are the dogs, those who practice magic arts, the sexually immoral, the murderers, the idolaters and everyone who loves and practices falsehood. I, Jesus, have sent my angel to give you this testimony for the churches. I am the Root and the Offspring of David, and the bright Morning Star (Rev 22:12–16).

The combined testimonies of these three figures—Peter, Paul, and Jesus—concerning Jesus as the Messiah are rehearsed by Martin Luther in his commentary on Galatians, where Luther, with the benefit of biblical revelation, demonstrated that all the promises of God effectively harken back to the first promise concerning Christ in Gen 3:15, that is, the one who would crush the serpent's head even as the serpent strikes at his heel:

> The faith of the fathers in the Old Testament era, and our faith in the New Testament are one and the same faith in Christ Jesus, although times and conditions may differ. Peter acknowledged this in the words: "Which neither our fathers nor we were able to bear? But we believe that through the grace of the Lord Jesus Christ we shall be saved, even as they" (Acts 15:10, 11). And Paul writes: "And did all drink the spiritual drink; for they drank of that spiritual Rock that followed them: and that Rock was Christ" (I Cor. 10:4). And Christ Himself declared: "Your father Abraham rejoiced to see my day: and he saw it and was glad" (John 8:56).[39]
> The faith of the fathers was directed at the Christ who was to come, while ours rests in the Christ who has come. Time does not change

---

39. Commenting on this same verse, John 8:56, Mike Mason has similarly argued that the messiahship of Christ Jesus is effectively confirmed by both the Old and New Testaments. As Mason has hypothesized about Eliphaz, one of Job's accusers, not being a true follower of Christ: "Denial of Christ may seem a bizarrely extreme charge to bring against an Old Testament figure, far in advance of the full revelation of the gospel. But the fact that every page of the Old Testament speaks of the coming of the Messiah, and the life of every true Old Testament believer in some way foreshadows, prepares for, or welcomes Christ's advent. Many even prophesy directly about Him. As Jesus noted in John 8:56, even Abraham 'rejoiced at the thought of seeing my day,' while of Moses it is written, 'He regarded disgrace for the sake of Christ as of greater value than the treasures of Egypt, because he was looking ahead to his reward' (Heb. 11:26). Simply put, the God of the Old Testament is Jesus Christ, and throughout the Bible the quintessence of true faith is the joyous embracing of the promise of Christ, however dimly perceived, and of the righteousness that only He can impart." Mason, *Gospel According to Job*, 75–76.

the object of true faith, or the Holy Spirit. There has always been and always will be one mind, one impression, one faith concerning Christ among true believers whether they live in times past, now, or in times to come. We too believe in the Christ to come as the fathers did in the Old Testament, for we look for Christ to come again on the day to judge the quick and the dead.[40]

The insistence that Jesus is the Christ as revealed throughout Scripture is also rendered by Augustine has been noted by Graham Ward:

> For Augustine the revelation of God's love, which is ultimately what is revealed by God of God, has its origin . . . in creation itself. The opening line of Genesis, "In the beginning," he interprets as "in Christ." So that in the historical incarnation Augustine's Christ comes into his own: As Word, creation came to be through Him. That he was not recognized was only a fault of human memory; a fault produced through sin.[41] If people, by a grace already given, could begin to understand what it was they truly desired, they would understand the God who had called them to be.[42]

Finally, for a statement of more recent vintage, we hear from the English journalist and writer Malcolm Muggeridge, who introduced the work of Mother Teresa to the Western world.[43] "Christ died on the cross as a man who had tried to show his fellowmen what life was about; he rose from the dead to be available to men forever as an intermediary between man and God," as Muggeridge, a former avowed atheist, declared. "What is not open to question is that today, two thousand years later, Christ is alive."[44]

---

40. Luther, *Commentary on St. Paul's Epistle to the Galatians*, 56.

41. As the apostle Paul wrote in his introduction to his epistle to the Romans, "The wrath of God is being revealed from heaven against all the godlessness and wickedness of people, who suppress the truth by their wickedness, since what may be known about God is plain to them, because God has made it plain to them. For since the creation of the world God's invisible qualities—his eternal power and divine nature—have been clearly seen, being understood from what has been made, so that people are without excuse. For although they knew God, they neither glorified him as God nor gave thanks to him, but their thinking became futile and their foolish hearts were darkened. Although they claimed to be wise, they became fools and exchanged the glory of the immortal God for images made to look like a mortal human being and birds and animals and reptiles" (Rom 1:18–23).

42. Ward, "Questioning God," 282.

43. Muggeridge, *Something Beautiful for God*.

44. Cited in Hunter, *Malcolm Muggeridge*, 227.

Are these varied instances of an insistent naming of Jesus and not another as the Christ tantamount to idolatry, as deconstruction likely warns? As we saw in the earlier chapters, any naming of Messiah is treated by deconstruction as a potential act in idolatry and possibly even injustice, which deconstruction works immediately and relentlessly to unsettle. Given deconstruction's suspicions against the metaphysics of presence and the work of naming that facilitates it, the Christian claim that only the name and person of Jesus matters understandably rankles. According to *Young's Analytical Concordance to the Bible*, the Hebrew variant of Jesus is Joshua ("Yah saves"), meaning, God saves and/or God rescues. Whenever the name of Jesus is invoked in praise or in prayer—as opposed to being done in vain (Exod 20:7)—it is a declaration, whether shouted in triumph from atop a mountain or whispered in one's final moments upon a deathbed, of our hope and desire that God saves, that he rescues and delivers, no more and no less. As Kevin Hart has reminded us, Christian faith properly understood consists in an open experience that must be reaffirmed in its irresolvable tension so long as it is lived, risked, and challenged.[45] It is neither a sacred code nor an ideological crutch, even if some religionists (like Job's three friends) inappropriately treat it as such. It is also noteworthy, for the writer of the book of Hebrews, that the place and role—as well as the *name*—of the incarnate Christ as the mainstay and manifestation of, and mouthpiece for God's progressive revelation were reserved specifically for the "last days":

> In the past God spoke to our ancestors through the prophets at many times and in various ways, but in these last days he has spoken to us by his Son, whom he appointed heir of all things, and through whom also he made the universe. The Son is the radiance of God's glory and the exact representation of his being, sustaining all things by his powerful word. After he had provided purification for sins, he sat down at the right hand of the Majesty in heaven. So he became as much superior to the angels as the name he has inherited is superior to theirs (Heb 1:1–4).

It is also worth recalling that the Christian's act of acknowledgment and affirmation of God is just as often a dialogical response to God conducted in the context of an ongoing relationship and conversation with him—in short, actions that take place amid spiritual encounters and experiences. These "first words" uttered by the Christ-follower are typically not

---

45. Hart, "Absolute Interruption," 197.

pronouncements of knowledge as much as acknowledgments regarding the presence and revelations of God and rejoinders to his invitations to conversation, communion, and collaboration with him. As the following exchanges suggest:

> When the LORD saw that he had gone over to look, God called to him from within the bush, "Moses! Moses!" And Moses said, "Here I am." "Do not come any closer," God said. "Take off your sandals, for the place where you are standing is holy ground." Then he said, "I am the God of your father, the God of Abraham, the God of Isaac and the God of Jacob." At this, Moses hid his face, because he was afraid to look at God (Exod 3:4–6).

> Then I heard the voice of the Lord saying, "Whom shall I send? And who will go for us?" And I said, "Here am I. Send me!" (Isa 6:8)

> The word of the LORD came to me, saying, "Before I formed you in the womb I knew you, before you were born I set you apart; I appointed you as a prophet to the nations." "Alas, Sovereign LORD," I said, "I do not know how to speak; I am too young." But the LORD said to me, "Do not say, 'I am too young.' You must go to everyone I send you to and say whatever I command you. Do not be afraid of them, for I am with you and will rescue you," declares the LORD (Jer 1:4–8).

In the above Scriptures, we see God initiating contact with his servants by way of a burning bush, a mystical vision, and a revealed word that invited and induced their responses—always given volitionally and never coerced.[46] At the burning bush encounter in Exod 3, God's command to Moses to keep his distance ("Do not come any closer") did not preclude God from making himself known to Moses in an intimate way ("I am the God of your father, the God of Abraham, the God of Isaac and the God of Jacob").[47] Granted, such encounters would typically reflect a growth in knowledge of God which arose from concrete experiences, say, God is named "provider" because he provided a sacrificial ram in place of

---

46. According to von Balthasar, "at the very center of the biblical events lies the Covenant between God and man, in which God gives man, whom he has created and endowed with freedom, an area of independent being, an area where he can freely hear and answer and ultimately cooperate responsibly with God . . . *His astounding masterpiece is to elicit the Yes of his free partner from the latter's innermost freedom.*" Von Balthasar, *Theo-Drama*, 34, italics mine.

47. Indeed, God would speak with Moses face-to-face as a man speaks with his friend (Exod 33:11).

Isaac (Gen 22:1–14), or God is named "healer" because he made the bitter water at Marah drinkable (Exod 15:22–26), and he is named "shepherd" for having guided and protected Israel not unlike how a good shepherd cares for her sheep (Ps 23). Yet these names do not connote the hermetical closure and narrow fixedness concerning the identity and meaning of God as much as an opening—for the God of the Bible is not just provider, healer, and shepherd, he is so much more. Crucially, these examples also illustrate the bidirectional quality of relational dynamics because conversation, communion, and collaboration with God equally mean that God initiates relationship with humankind as well as responds to its invocation of his name: Jesus! God saves! Indeed, God typically initiates well before any naming takes place: "But before there is even any discussion of naming, before Moses asks Who shall I say sent me?, God tells Moses that he is the one who *hears* and knows of the Israelites' affliction," as Regina Schwartz observes in her analysis of the encounter between God and Moses in Exod 3. "Indeed, this is why he appears to Moses, to say *he has heard and seen and means to save* . . . hearing, seeing, and saving are versions of the same act: response."[48]

The God of the Bible hears, sees, speaks, acts, calls, names, and replies. As Moses discovered in his burning bush encounter, any naming that does take place usually involves God first calling to us and naming us in the process—before we even know him! As Paul testified about his conversion before Agrippa and Bernice at Caesarea:

> On one of these journeys I was going to Damascus with the authority and commission of the chief priests. About noon, King Agrippa, as I was on the road, I saw a light from heaven, brighter than the sun, blazing around me and my companions. We all fell to the ground, and I heard a voice saying to me in Aramaic, "Saul, Saul, why do you persecute me? It is hard for you to kick against the goads." Then I asked, "Who are you, Lord?" "I am Jesus, whom you are persecuting," the Lord replied. "Now get up and stand on your feet. I have appeared to you to appoint you as a servant and as a witness of what you have seen and will see of me" (Acts 26:12–16).

These instances of our calling to and naming of God, as Martin Buber and Franz Rosenzweig separately reminded us, are better regarded not as intellectual exercises in metaphysics and ontotheology as much as

---

48. Schwartz, "Questioning Narratives of God," 219, italics original.

acknowledgments in response to historically lived experiences.[49] Referencing the prophet Isaiah's response to God in Isa 6:8, Simon Critchley has proposed the following riposte to metaphysics: "my first word is not Descartes' 'ego cogito' ('I am, I think'), it is rather 'me voici!' ('here I am!' or 'see me here!'), the word with which the prophet testifies to the presence of God."[50] Called and confronted by God, one does not analyze and theorize; rather, one either acknowledges and responds to the call, or walks away from it altogether. As the Catholic theologian Hans Urs von Balthasar put it, "For God's revelation is not an object to be looked at: it is his action in and upon the world, and the world can only respond, and hence 'understand,' through action on *its* part."[51] Critchley's observation underscores the obvious: we risk slipping into metaphysics—and, with that, potentially into the idolatry of which deconstruction warns us—whenever we depart from first words and the immediacy of dialogical interaction with God. Presumably, we are only able to avoid this pitfall by sticking closely to the terms of relationship as defined by Jesus: *Remain in me, as I also remain in you* (John 15:4a), which keeps us in a state of constant interaction and intimacy with Christ whilst preventing any insidious distancing away from God. In this respect, Kevin Hart is surely correct to insist that Christ-followers rightly reside in a space of acknowledgment rather than of knowledge, where the conjunction of faith and reason never resolves itself in favor of knowledge because God eludes all human and institutional attempts at ideological capture and domestication.[52] Aporias are very much part and parcel of the life of faith, where the Christian's spiritual experience of desire, intuition, gratitude, and wonder—and yes, including puzzlement and exasperation—always exceed the bounds of theological knowledge.[53] In his discussion of creation faith, Walter Brueggemann makes a similar point:

49. Bowler, "Rosenzweig on Judaism and Christianity," and Buber, *Moses*.
50. Critchley, "Introduction," 22.
51. Von Balthasar, *Theo-Drama*, 15, italics original.
52. According to Hart, "*We live in a space of acknowledgment, not knowledge.* The old conjunction of "faith and reason" never resolves itself in favor of knowledge. Augustine speaks of seeking understanding, not knowing. One lives, or tries to live, in the trace of God, which in its deepest sense is the trace of the Trinity . . . When we love each other, as Jesus taught us, we are letting the *basileia* [kingdom of God] break into the world. In loving each other, the Trinity has passed through us as a trace." Hart, "Absolute Interruption," 202, italics mine.
53. As Hart writes, "When one accepts the free gift of faith, nothing is thereby made simple. Not at all: One's experience as a Christian is always structured as what you call an aporia. We have to try to balance an absolute trust in God with the relative historical

It is enough to acknowledge, be awed, and delighted. This incredible past, to which we have only lyrical access [i.e., via the biblical narrative], pushes one's *raison d'être* out beyond one's self, thus quickly refusing every notion of self-sufficiency and suiting us for an Other with whom we have by definition to do . . . That I exist is a reality that is referred to outside myself to the mystery of God to which I can only respond in gratitude and doxology. Because I exist, I must sing a song that voices my life in unfettered gratitude.[54]

Such a response to God as that proposed by Brueggemann above is one that deconstruction neither recognizes nor permits because of its nondenominational commitment to not name or specify.[55] According to Caputo, Derrida's "religion," so to speak, "is very un-denominational, by keeping a safe distance not only between itself and any of the concrete messianisms (Christian, Jewish, Islamic) of the religions of the book, but also between itself and any monetary denominations, that is, economies—whereas Marion is interested in a very Christian economy."[56] But is deconstruction right to insist that unnameability and unknowability—including a messiah who must never show up—comprise the best measures of impossibility? Time and again the God of the Bible is presented as a God who boasts a track record of having achieved impossible feats, or at least claims to have the ability and the authority to do such things (e.g., Jer 32:27; Matt 19:26; Mark 10:27). And the Christian's response to this is to declare praise of and to his God, even Christ: "Now to him who is able to do immeasurably more than all we ask or imagine, according to his power that is at work within us, to him be glory in the church and in Christ Jesus throughout all generations, for ever and ever! Amen" (Eph 3:20–21).

---

knowledge we have about the life, suffering, and death of Jesus. We have to hold an incalculable revelation of divine love in tandem with the calculations involved in revealability. We have to keep the contrary tugs of faith and reason in some sort of relation, and we never emerge securely from that situation: It pushes us on, ever on, though without any positive assurance because we are pulled even more deeply into a mystery. Christian experience does not neatly resolve itself into knowledge: A good deal of it remains desire, intuition, wonder, puzzlement." Hart, "Absolute Interruption," 202.

54. Brueggemann, *Texts Under Negotiation*, 29–30.

55. As Levinas put it, "The Bible is the priority of the other [*l'autre*] in relation to me. It is in another [*autrui*] that I always see the widow and the orphan. The other [*autrui*] always comes first. This is what I've called, in Greek language, the dissymmetry of the interpersonal relationship. If there is not this dissymmetry, then no line of what I've written can hold. And this is vulnerability. Only a vulnerable I can love his neighbor." Levinas, *Of God Who Comes to Mind*, 85.

56. Caputo, "Apostles of the Impossible," 198.

Hello from the Other Side

A Tale of Two "Waits"

> But as for me, I watch in hope for the Lord, I wait for God my Savior; my God will hear me (Mic 7:7).

> Christ has died, Christ is risen, Christ will come again.
> —The Memorial Acclamation

In fairness to Derrida and deconstruction, a key distinctive that informs their wait for the messianic, as we have seen, involves a God who is always structurally *to come*. In Derrida's 1999 debate with the Catholic theologian Jean-Luc Marion, it became clear that while both thinkers agreed on many things, the fundamental issue that divided them had to do with Derrida's insistence on a messiah that is still to come and Marion's belief in a messiah "who has already pitched his tent among us in the flesh."[57] And while Derrida's deep admiration for Augustine of Hippo's profound honesty—"What do I love when I love my God?"—was arguably what inspired him to pen his own confessional statement, "Circumfession,"[58] he nonetheless differed from the latter in that while both men rendered their impossible decisions amid shared conditions of ineradicable undecidability, Augustine unequivocally placed his bets on the determinate historical Jesus as Messiah whereas Derrida deliberately left the door open on what or who Messiah might turn out to be, if he/she/it were to come at all. Far from a situation where Augustine decided but Derrida did not, could not, or would not decide, both men rendered and sustained their respective decisions in the face of an undecidability that persisted before, during, and after their decisions.[59]

In this respect, Derrida's differences with both Marion and Augustine could be presented in terms of two different forms of waiting, namely, a waiting *for* and a waiting *on*. Much like Derrida and deconstruction, Christ-followers await the return of their Messiah; "Christ has died, Christ is risen, Christ will come again," as Christians recite per the liturgy of the Eucharist. But as we have seen, deconstruction is waiting *for* a God that can neither be known nor named; indeed, it is a God who can never come because if he/she/it did come, what else then is there to wait and live for? As for Christ-followers, their wait, deconstruction is wont to say, is not really a

---

57. Caputo and Scanlon, "Introduction," 15.
58. Derrida, "Circumfession."
59. Caputo, "What Do I Love When I Love My God?" 312.

real wait since the Christian claim is Messiah who has already come in the form of the incarnate Christ, a savior who is already with us—Immanuel, God with us (Matt 1:23)—rather than one who is still to come. That said, it could be asked of Christianity's waiting *on* its Messiah, reportedly already known and named, who is due to return soon: Will Jesus who is to come again going to arrive in the same form as he did, in human form, over two thousand years ago? This seems like a crucially important question in view of deconstruction's insistence that Christianity's anticipation of Parousia, the second coming of Christ, is not a legitimate advent because that which Christians await is not the impossible but the already possible—a God already given, known, named, and hence wholly domesticated and mythologized.[60] As Caputo has observed, "For Derrida the presence of God is the coming of God, and the gift of God is a gift without givenness, *le don sans la donation*, not a gift of givenness but a faith in the gift to come."[61] Stated differently, any expectation of a gift of givenness—one already defined and delimited, one already known and named—can only be understood, as we saw earlier, as part of a totalizing teleology which deconstruction has warned regarding Christian eschatology.

But does the Parousia insist on a complete givenness without surprises, nothing that would shock and awe even (or especially) those who pray without ceasing, "Maranatha"? If anything, Christian eschatology, when properly practiced in the context of biblical faith, prevents an open-ended and vibrant eschatology from stultifying into a totalized teleology. Consider, for example, Brueggemann's reflection on the link between biblical faith and eschatology:

> The dramatic power of biblical faith is that it is, in large sweep, ordered into a past/present/future, that is, with a life *created* by God and *consummated* by God. This is such a truism in the community of faith that I think we often fail to see how very odd such a claim is, and how crucial it is for the good news of the gospel. It is both odd and crucial when this pattern of affirmation is contrasted

---

60. As Caputo has argued, "In the end, Derrida wants to save those precious names, of God and the gift, and he daily prays and weeps for a Messiah to come and save both them and us . . . In just the way the Other who is given is not the Other, so the gift which is given is not the gift, and . . . the God who is given is not God. God, the gift and the *tout autre* share a common trait: They are each annulled from the moment they appear or are given, so that if they appear or are given then we may be sure that what appeared was not God, the gift, or the *tout autre*." Caputo, "Apostles of the Impossible," 205–06, 208.

61. Caputo, "Apostles of the Impossible," 200.

with the primary propensity of modern secularism, which believes in neither a creation nor a consummation. The result of the banishment of an ultimate past and future in the modern world, that is, creation and consummation, is that the present is taken with inordinate and uncritical seriousness, if not absolutized.[62]

The ability to think in eschatological terms, and to live in accordance with it, is well encapsulated in Richard Kearney's notion of a "historical hermeneutic" and, so argued, its mitigating effect against contrasting totalizations, namely, the equally problematic claims of positivistic immutability, on the one hand, and of postmodern variability on the other:

> [A historical hermeneutic] is one capable of imagining what things might be like *after* postmodernism. And also, of course, what things were like *before* it. As such, the ethical imagination explodes the paralysis of a timeless present, cultivated by our contemporary culture, and informs us that humanity has a duty, if it wishes to survive its threatened ending, to remember the past and to project a future. We cannot even begin to *know* what the postmodern present is unless we are first prepared to *imagine* what it has been and what it *may become*. To abandon this imaginative potential for historical *depth* is to surrender to a new positivism which declares that things are the way they are and cannot be altered; it is tantamount to embracing the postmodern cult of 'euphoric surfaces' which dissolves the critical notions of authenticity, alienation, and anxiety in a dazzling rain of 'discontinuous, orgasmic instances.'"[63]

Thus understood, Christian eschatology anticipates the return of Messiah—the Jesus who has come, and hence known, named, and familiar, but whose imminent return bears hints of newness, unfamiliarity, and unpredictability. The biblical narrative seems to suggest that the Jesus to come is not quite the same as the Jesus who has already come, whether by dint of his role and function or even, quite literally in superficial terms, his looks. Memorably, the one who has already come announced his entrance, in the synagogue at Nazareth, by reading the first two verses of Isa 61—effectively ending his public reading at the words, "to proclaim the year of the Lord's favor" (Isa 61:2a)—and added this astonishing declaration, "Today this scripture is fulfilled in your hearing" (Luke 4:21). That Jesus did not peruse

---

62. Brueggemann, *Texts Under Negotiation*, 28, italics original.

63. Kearney, "Ethics and the Postmodern Imagination," 52–53, cited in Brueggemann, *Texts Under Negotiation*, 28–29.

the part of the text that says, "the day of vengeance of our God" (Isa 61:2b) implies the prospect of another advent involving the one who is to come—a time of divine judgment (Acts 10:42; Acts 17:31; Rom 2:16), where the Messiah would return not primarily as the Lamb of God who died for the sins of the world, but as the Lion of Judah, the all-conquering King of kings and Lord of lords. The God of the Bible is full of surprises and "new things"; it bears reminding that he is no one-trick pony given to doing the same thing or relying on the same method again and again, as if he were stuck in some Nietzschean warp of eternal recurrence:

> This is what the LORD says—he who made a way through the sea, a path through the mighty waters, who drew out the chariots and horses, the army and reinforcements together, and they lay there, never to rise again, extinguished, snuffed out like a wick: "Forget the former things; do not dwell on the past. See, I am doing a new thing! Now it springs up; do you not perceive it? I am making a way in the wilderness and streams in the wasteland" (Isa 43:16–19).

In their efforts to reconcile the contrasting images of the suffering servant and the victorious messiah, some Talmudic writers have gone as far as to construct the notion of two distinct messiahs—one known as Messiah ben Joseph, because he would suffer, and the other known as Messiah ben David, because he would be victorious over the nations in battle and reign as king over the whole earth.[64] As Raphael Patai has explained:

> When the death of the Messiah became an established tenet in Talmudic times, this was felt to be irreconcilable with the belief in Messiah as the Redeemer who would usher in the blissful millennium of the Messianic age. The dilemma was solved by splitting the person of the Messiah in two; one of them, called Messiah ben Joseph, was to raise the armies of Israel against their enemies, and, after many victories and miracles, would fall victim to Gog and Magog. The other, Messiah ben David, will come after him . . . and will lead Israel to the ultimate victory, the triumph, and the Messianic era of bliss.[65]

The scriptural passages most often cited in support of the notion of two distinct messiahs are from the book of Zechariah. The first, from Zech 9, recalls the suffering servant of Isa 53 who was led like a lamb to the slaughter and who kept silent despite his oppression and affliction:

---

64. Dix, "Messiah Ben Joseph."
65. Patai, *Messiah Texts*, 166.

> Rejoice greatly, Daughter Zion! Shout, Daughter Jerusalem! See, your king comes to you, righteous and victorious, lowly and riding on a donkey, on a colt, the foal of a donkey. I will take away the chariots from Ephraim and the warhorses from Jerusalem, and the battle bow will be broken. He will proclaim peace to the nations. His rule will extend from sea to sea and from the River to the ends of the earth (Zech 9:9–10).

The second, from Zech 14, evokes the majestic Lord from Ps 2 who, far from silent like the suffering servant, laughs and scoffs at the nations arrayed against him, and rebukes them in his anger and terrifies them in his wrath:

> Then the LORD will go out and fight against those nations, as he fights on a day of battle. On that day his feet will stand on the Mount of Olives, east of Jerusalem, and the Mount of Olives will be split in two from east to west, forming a great valley, with half of the mountain moving north and half moving south . . . On that day living water will flow out from Jerusalem, half of it east to the Dead Sea and half of it west to the Mediterranean Sea, in summer and in winter. The LORD will be king over the whole earth. On that day there will be one LORD, and his name the only name (Zech 14:3–4, 8–9).

Nor, it would appear, do the two messiahs look alike. Writing about five hundred years before the birth of Jesus, the prophet Daniel described the divine vision he received:

> In my vision at night I looked, and there before me was one like a son of man, coming with the clouds of heaven. He approached the Ancient of Days and was led into his presence. He was given authority, glory and sovereign power; all nations and peoples of every language worshiped him. His dominion is an everlasting dominion that will not pass away, and his kingdom is one that will never be destroyed (Dan 7:13–14).

Conceivably, the "one like a son of man" on whom Daniel laid eyes could have looked exactly like Jesus did to Peter and the disciples, five centuries later by the shores of the Sea of Galilee. However, on his part, the apostle John, who was very clear about the source of his revelation as none other than the incarnate Christ with whom he spent three years of every waking moment (Rev 1:1–2), nonetheless described a fantastical image that bore little resemblance to the man against whose bosom he once reclined (John 13:23):

> I turned around to see the voice that was speaking to me. And when I turned I saw seven golden lampstands, and among the lampstands was someone like a son of man, dressed in a robe reaching down to his feet and with a golden sash around his chest. The hair on his head was white like wool, as white as snow, and his eyes were like blazing fire. His feet were like bronze glowing in a furnace, and his voice was like the sound of rushing waters. In his right hand he held seven stars, and coming out of his mouth was a sharp, double-edged sword. His face was like the sun shining in all its brilliance (Rev 1:12–16).

Are the Messiah who has come (the suffering servant riding a borrowed donkey in Matt 21:5) and the one who is to come (the sovereign king and judge on his white horse in Rev 19:11) one and the same? The book of Revelation seems determined to underscore the fact that the second advent constitutes not the coming of another but the return of one who had previously come, Jesus, but in a somewhat different form and with a different function—or, if you like, "same, same but different," as the title of a popular children's book has it.[66] Their differences could be sufficiently extensive to the point that there is no legitimate reason to insist that the Christ who will soon return looks, talks, and acts exactly like the incarnate Christ from two thousand years ago. Put differently, to declare that "Christ has died, Christ is risen, Christ will come again" is not to claim full and complete knowledge of the Christ who will return as the conquering king. Indeed, the likelihood is that he may be unrecognizable to many—including those who call themselves Christians—because not everyone who says to him, "Lord, Lord," will enter the kingdom of heaven, but only those who do the will of his heavenly Father (Matt 7:21–23). Such an explanation is unlikely to satisfy deconstruction's conditions for otherness, for which any "same yet different" logic amounts to an attempt at reconciliation and resolution, and therefore remains for all intents and purposes a claim about the perdurability of metaphysical essence. After all, all Christian theology—whether cataphatic, negative, or mystical, or still some other—is, in deconstruction's view, always going about the heavenly Father's business, as it were, and seeking to preserve his preeminence.

---

66. Kostecki-Shaw, *Same, Same But Different*.

Christian Witness, A.D. (After Deconstruction)

All said, deconstruction, as we have seen, has much to offer the Christ-follower by way of good counsel. At the most basic level, it is likely that Christian testimony in the postmodern era can no longer be presented in the way it used to be done.[67] Christians must certainly continue to share the love and truth of Christ with their neighbors, although we do so no longer with the myopic false confidence of the modern past, especially not when our testimony is confronted daily with a pervasive skepticism that no longer permits us the luxury of articulating truth in modernity's categories and grammar. In other words, we certainly, we must, continue to testify about God, but with assurance in Christ rather than the certitude understood and insisted by modernity. Put another way, the present zeitgeist has given us the license and permission to be more honest with our doubts, difficulties, and fears, that is, our honest acknowledgment of the aporias and undecidability within which our Christian faith and life take place. Not unlike the example furnished by Job, integrity before God and our fellowmen is what ultimately counts, despite the unhelpful presence of certain "friends"—the contemporary equivalent of Eliphaz, Bildad, and Zophar—who continually impose on us their modernist, one-dimensional caricatures of God and fixed formulas on faith and reason where knowledge, and a highly flawed one at that, always triumphs gratitude and acknowledgment. Indeed, it bears reminding that the apostle Matthew did not mince words when describing the state of his fellow disciples when the Eleven met the resurrected Christ immediately prior to his ascension into heaven: "When they saw him, they worshiped him; *but some doubted*" (Matt 28:17, italics mine). In Caputo's words:

> [T]here is an atheist in the heart of every believer, who haunts and taunts the believer with disbelief, even if there is a believer in the heart of every atheist or agnostic, haunting and taunting them with God, and the two are always fighting. To "be" a believer or an atheist is to live with that dissension within ourselves. Derrida's formula is a good one, not only for himself, but for all of

---

67. Absent the relatively stable stock of Judeo-Christian norms and values that undergirded Western societies in times past, work stressing the Gospel's "bigness"—one that emphasizes relatedness to all areas of life—is needed to "level the playing field," as it were, through a vigilant engagement with the epistemological and ontological assumptions and prejudices held by postmodern audiences; or, a la Francis Schaeffer, "taking the roof off" the postmodern worldview. Newman, *Bringing the Gospel Home*, 139.

us, mutatis mutandis, for the faithful would do very well to say of themselves not that they "are" but that they "rightly pass for" Christians or Jews, Muslims or Hindus, not unlike the way that Johannes Climacus, given the "difficulty" of a being a Christian, preferred to speak of "becoming" Christian rather than of being one. We do not know who we are or what is to come, and we are more than one.[68]

In a poem written just weeks before he was executed by the Nazis for his opposition to Hitler's regime, the German pastor and theologian Dietrich Bonhoeffer provided this painfully honest self-portrait of inner turmoil in contrast to the pillar of strength for which his fellow inmates, as well as the prison guards, regarded him:

> Am I then really that which other men tell of?
> Or am I only what I myself know of myself?
> Restless and longing and sick, like a bird in a cage,
> Struggling for breath, as though hands were compressing my throat,
> Yearning for colors, for flowers, for the voices of birds,
> Thirsting for words of kindness, for neighborliness,
> Tossing in expectations of great events,
> Powerlessly trembling for friends at an infinite distance,
> Weary and empty at praying, at thinking, at making,
> Faint, and ready to say farewell to it all.
> Who am I? This or the Other?
> Am I one person today and tomorrow another?
> Am I both at once? A hypocrite before others,
> And before myself a contemptible woebegone weakling?
> Or is something within me still like a beaten army
> Fleeing in disorder from victory already achieved?
> Who am I? They mock me, these lonely questions of mine.
> Whoever I am, Thou Knowest, O God, I am thine![69]

In the same way, we too are assailed incessantly by a litany of searching questions posed to us—not only by deconstruction, but life itself with all of its complexities and challenges—that cross-examine and even mock the supposed surety of our Christian faith and testimony. However, contra deconstruction's suspicion against Christianity's concrete messianism, we who are on this difficult pilgrimage of "becoming Christian" must nonetheless determine, in faith, to walk in obedience to Christ—to follow Jesus

---

68. Caputo, "What Do I Love When I Love My God?" 309.
69. Bonhoeffer, *Who Am I?*

amid aporia and undecidability—and to keep sharing the truth of his hope in word and deed. Remarkably, as Matthew described it, that some among the Eleven doubted the risen Christ did not prevent *all* of them, including the doubters, from worshiping him, however. After all, is not our worship of, our belief in, and our service to and for God *amid doubt* the very embodiment of an active and biblically grounded faith? In the words of the apostle James:

> You foolish person, do you want evidence that faith without deeds is useless? Was not our father Abraham considered righteous for what he did when he offered his son Isaac on the altar? You see that his faith and his actions were working together, and his faith was made complete by what he did. And the scripture was fulfilled that says, "Abraham believed God, and it was credited to him as righteousness," and he was called God's friend. You see that a person is considered righteous by what they do and not by faith alone. In the same way, was not even Rahab the prostitute considered righteous for what she did when she gave lodging to the spies and sent them off in a different direction? As the body without the spirit is dead, so faith without deeds is dead (Jas 2:20–26).

Against deconstruction's commitment to an endless wait for a God whose advent deconstruction would prefer not to be realized, the followers of Jesus decide amid doubt and undecidability to deny themselves, pick up their crosses, and follow him (Luke 9:23). In a postmodern world replete with a thousand ambiguities and uncertainties, the only assurance one has regarding one's life of faith is whether God sees and knows her (Matt 7:21–23); the Lord is "the God who sees me," as Sarah's handmaiden, Hagar, named him (Gen 16:13).

Arguably, all this has implications for our Christian witness in the postmodern age, where the biblical injunction to speak the truth about God in love (in Eph 4:15) may best be expressed as a gentle and humble witness that honestly, courageously, and patiently engages with deconstruction rather than shy away from being cross-examined by it. As Brueggemann has allowed, "The cross-examination will not defeat the testimony . . . probably. But it will cause the testimony to be issued in a sobered, trembling voice."[70]

---

70. Brueggemann, *Theology of the Old Testament*, 332. In like fashion, notwithstanding Paul's knowledge of Christ in whom he believed and the confidence he had that Christ would guard that which Paul had entrusted to him (2 Tim 1:12), the apostle's counsel to Christ-followers is to continue to work out their salvation in fear and trembling (Phil 2:12).

This in no way denies let alone disparages deconstruction; rather, Derrida's dedication to the "undeconstructible"—to truth and justice, for example, even "God"—should be welcomed, encouraged, and applauded, driven as it has been by his desire to affirm and embrace life. In Caputo's words, "Derrida's love, no less than Augustine's, is a love of truth, of doing the truth, *facere veritatem*."[71] Indeed, it could be said that the position taken by Derrida and deconstruction is similar to that of Aristotle, who famously averred in the *Nichomachean Ethics*, "Plato is my friend, but truth is a better friend" (*Amicus Plato, sed magis amica veritas*).[72] This is something with which Christians can identify; as Jesus, who declared himself as the "the way and the truth and the life" (John 14:6), also informed Pilate, "the reason I was born and came into the world is to testify to the truth. Everyone on the side of truth listens to me" (John 18:37b). As Robert Vallie, in his comparative analysis of Derrida and Augustine, has rightly noted:

> Truth is not something we produce. Instead, in a certain manner of speaking, we are productions of truth. Truth haloes us and prods us to attain a deeper ontological depth. By living in the truth, one's horizon is expanded and made more fecund. We grow in the truth; the truth does not grow in us. Like pygmies blindly grappling with the elephant god, we never exhaust, or even fully grasp, the object of our knowing. Therefore, the art of knowing is a perpetual and fully human struggle to dwell in truth.[73]

In so many ways, the honest pursuit of Christ bears remarkable similarities to deconstruction's own quest for truth. However, in its refusal to lay down the cross of undecidability—by deciding to stay indefinitely within the state of undecidability and agnosticism—deconstruction, for all intents and purposes, appears to have made its pragmatic choice against following Christ. But here too we are confronted by the faith-riveted commitment of Dostoevsky, who once insisted, "If someone proved to me that Christ is outside the truth and that *in reality*, the truth were outside of Christ, then I should prefer to remain with Christ rather than with the truth."[74] As we have

---

71. Caputo, What Do I Love When I Love My God?" 312.

72. Or that of Isaac Newton, who reportedly paraphrased off Aristotle: "Plato is my friend; Aristotle is my friend, but my greatest friend is truth."

73. Vallie, "Augustine Confessions," 49.

74. Cited in Frank, *Dostoevsky*, 712, italics original. Granted, Dostoevsky's statement, or at least the logic behind it, could just as easily be (mis)appropriated by religionists to reject knowledge that they consider, rightly or otherwise, as worldly and/or ungodly. It is perhaps fair to say that some "Christian" responses to the coronavirus pandemic suggest

seen, the biblical narrative is chockfull of stories of godly women and men who, when confronted by commonsensical knowledge and worldly wisdom that reject and ridicule the seemingly fantastical nature of the biblical God and his promises and prophecies, chose nonetheless to believe in him—a reluctant grizzled leader leading God's people out of slavery, three young Hebrew men unsinged by the molten blaze of a heathen king's furnace, elderly couples producing children, a virgin who bears the promised son of God, the dead coming back to life, the list goes on. These too are decisions rendered amid undecidability—the decision of the follower of Jesus to say yes to life in Christ.

---

the readiness by some to use God's name—possibly in vain, in some instances—to reject sound policy guidelines aimed at protecting the American public from the virus. On the other hand, not all policy advice has been well thought through and formulated before implementation, which has only added more confusion to an already complex and difficult situation.

Conclusion
Homecoming in Christ

> Whoever wants to be my disciple must deny themselves and take up their cross daily and follow me. For whoever wants to save their life will lose it, but whoever loses their life for me will save it. What good is it for someone to gain the whole world, and yet lose or forfeit their very self? (Luke 9:23–25)

> That is, my first word is not Descartes' "ego cogito" ("I am, I think"), it is rather "me voici!" ("here I am!" or "see me here!"), the word with which the prophet [Isaiah] testifies to the presence of God.[1]

THIS BOOK HAS SOUGHT to chart my inquiry, by way of a dialogue with Derridean deconstruction, about the conditions of hospitality toward otherness, specifically the divine Other, God. In his own fashion, Jacques Derrida, the consummate champion of deconstruction, was similarly interested in the holy and the messianic, his professed atheism vis-à-vis the orthodox faiths notwithstanding. With deconstruction as his weapon—think, for instance, of the sharp sword emanating from Christ's mouth with which he used to strike down enemies left and right (Rev 19:15)—Derrida was on a knightly quest to wage discursive/textual wars on all manners of perceived idolatry and injustice, particularly those perpetrated by institutions that profess to be on the side of truth and justice, often in the name of God. Like his namesake Elijah facing off against an army of false prophets atop Carmel, Jackie Élie Derrida was a holy warrior engaged in holy work. That said, Derrida's and deconstruction's work of demythologization was conducted neither on behalf of any orthodox faith and concrete messianism,

---

1. Critchley, "Introduction," 22.

Conclusion

least of all Christianity, nor of a known/knowable and named/namable God, least of all Jesus of Nazareth. Rather, deconstruction treats anything that claims to represent the holy and the messianic as participating, willfully or otherwise, in the metaphysics of presence and thereby engaging in idolatry. Accordingly, even apophatic/negative theology, which presents God as ineffable and mysterious, would not do because theologians of *via negativa* are ultimately going about the business of the Christian God and seeking to preserve his eminence. Significantly, it was not only metaphysical considerations that concerned Derrida, but the rampant hypocrisies and blood-soaked histories of concrete messianisms that, for Derrida, made a complete mockery of their professed religiosity and piety. In its own way, deconstruction is resolutely dedicated to affirming life—to saying yes to life, just not life *in Christ*.

I began this book, in the first chapter, by appealing against the proclivity in a "self before other" understanding, one that privileges and prioritizes a notion of self that resists alterity and otherness, blind to its inherent indebtedness to the latter. I suggested that should even a religious quest for desire and destiny be grounded in just such a conception of self, its outcome is likely to be limited to a sort of homecoming where self can only beget self with little meaningful change. As Merold Westphal has observed, "Behind what professes to be love of God and neighbor they regularly find love of self, disguised beyond recognition, at least to those who perpetuate this pious fraud."[2] In contrast to the dubious motives and manner with which some Christians, intentionally or otherwise, have engaged in the formation of self, the Bible's understanding of self-discovery and homecoming is different than that in other sources, classical and contemporary. We considered the cases of Inman and Odysseus, who aimed to return home to their loved ones and places of origin, respectively. By contrast, the biblical patriarch Abraham was told by God to depart his native land and go without looking back, without hope of going back (Gen 12:1). Unlike Inman and Odysseus, Abraham was not invited to find himself by cultivating a nostalgia for his past. Rather—and here, against Derrida's normative appeal, I follow the Christological interpretation of Søren Kierkegaard, in *Fear and Trembling*, of the life of Abraham the "knight of faith"—Abraham could only find his true self and his calling in God by paradoxically denying self, losing his life, bearing his cross, and following God, as Jesus enjoined his disciples in Luke 9:23 (cf. Matt 16:24). Indeed, that his name

---

2. Westphal, *Suspicion and Faith*, 9.

was changed by God from Abram to Abraham—from "exalted father" to "father of many nations" (Gen 17:5)—reflects at the very least the divine promise and human prospect of impending radical transformation of identity and interest. That Abraham refused the temptation to take short cuts in his quest is evidenced by his decision not to settle in Haran but to proceed to Canaan in response to the call of the Other, even though he took occasional wrong turns and did not know where he was headed (Heb 11:8). Such a pilgrimage involved a willingness on his part to forgo everything he had, including his very self; as Peter exclaimed to Christ, "We have left everything to follow you!" (Matt 19:27). As Catherine Chalier has noted:

> Abraham discovers his integrity as a man called to be a blessing to all families of the earth, only on condition that he loses himself, that is, only on condition that he gets rid of all that which, by keeping him prisoner of his past—words, images, possessions—would make impossible for him the going forward to the Promised Land. It is the land to which he none the less proceeds, day after day, for his entire humanity lies in his answer to the call he heard.[3]

Derrida also recognized this to be the case. "Here there is no return," he wrote of Abraham's pilgrimage. "For desire is not unhappy. It is opening and freedom."[4] Put differently, there is no real journey or pilgrimage of which to speak so long as one resists or refuses to relinquish self, especially a conception of self that regards itself as always and already determined and settled. This does not mean that such a self would necessarily be resistant to change. But any change it is able and willing to make is likely to be limited and kept within its own inscribed bounds of identity and interest, with minimal effort expended and where no agonizing "dark nights of the soul"—no spiritual crisis in the journey toward (comm)union with God—need apply. On the other hand, a pilgrimage that takes seriously the absolute sovereign Other as its desire and destiny will likely lead one to crises of belief but also great victories, for such are the lot of journeys in faith—journeys that are never grounded in and/or initiated by ourselves (i.e., the "ego cogito" of Descartes) but happen in response (i.e., the "me voici!" of Isaiah) to the invitation from, the command of, our Creator-God.[5] How one moves from a Cartesian self-centered quest to Isaiah's God-shaped self, born of

---

3. Chalier, "Levinas and the Talmud," 106.
4. Derrida, "Violence and Metaphysics," 93.
5. Critchley, "Introduction," 202.

CONCLUSION

her response to the call placed on her by the absolute and sovereign Other, is the heart of the matter.

Deconstruction provides a way toward otherness. In the second and third chapters, we were introduced briefly to the philosophy of deconstruction and its purposes and practices. We noted, contra the common and unfair dismissal of deconstruction as philosophically relativistic and morally nihilistic by critics who likely formed their views within echo chambers of cliched and unreliable secondhand opinions, that deconstruction, at least in Derrida's hands, is not against faith and religion as such but seeks to salvage it. The paradigm of deconstruction, as John Caputo reminded us, is the idea of "a Messiah who is never to show," and because of this constant deferral of his/her/its advent, it makes the seeker long and desire it even more.[6] By this logic, deconstruction is not, as its critics insist, the dismantlement and destruction, wanton and willy-nilly, of things; it is not an uncontrollable tornado that leaves nothing but wreckage in its trail. Rather, as Gayatri Spivak has put it, deconstruction is the critique of things that are extremely helpful, without which we cannot do anything,[7] without which life would be impossible. Accordingly, deconstruction happens because every good and helpful thing—spiritual faith and its facilitating institutions, for instance—is engendered through processes of exclusion and repression. But despite systematic and violent efforts to keep them buried and hidden, repressed things have a way of returning, unbidden, to haunt its oppressors. More times than not, it is those hidden truths that bring real life and freedom; think, for example, of the wrath Jesus reserved for the Pharisees and religious teachers who worked hard to keep God's liberating truth out of the people's hands, just so they and their fellow religious elites in Jerusalem could maintain their power and privilege under their Roman colonizers. Indeed, it may not be untoward to view Jesus as a master deconstructionist without equal![8] Hence deconstruction's relentless quest to smash all idols and to war against all injustices until it encounters the real thing—the event, to borrow from Deleuze—that finally defies dismantlement. Hence Derrida's firm insistence that deconstruction has always been affirmative in orientation and has always sought to deliver an unqualified

---

6. Caputo, "Apostles of the Impossible," 186.
7. Cited in Butler, *Bodies That Matter*, 27.
8. Caputo, *What Would Jesus Deconstruct?*

yes to life.⁹ Deconstruction is not God and does not claim to be God,¹⁰ but, perhaps not unlike the role of wisdom in the Scriptures (Prov 4:5–9, 8:22–23), works in the service of deconstruction's Messiah to clear paths toward the holy and the messianic by leveling mountains, raising valleys, and paving the highway to holiness (Isa 40:3–4).

By the same token, deconstruction keeps confronting a huge bugbear in its labors, namely, Derrida's concrete messianisms. All claims by the orthodox religions (or by religious cults and sects, for that matter) that Messiah has come are to be treated with skepticism and suspicion—are to be deconstructed—because claims that the divine is known/knowable and named/namable are deemed idolatrous to the extent they are exercises in metaphysics.¹¹ For its troubles, deconstruction found ready sympathizers among Christian thinkers worried over the objectification and rationalization of religion to the extent that the worship of God and Christ becomes (mis)treated as a *Baalism redivivus*.¹² But deconstruction does not stop there. Recall that Derrida's conception of the messianic is something that or someone who is never to show at all because the nonappearance of the Messiah is for Derrida a way to protect us against idols. Hence deconstruction's insistence that no crossover to the *tout autre* or wholly other is ever conceivable because should that ever happen—God forbid, deconstruction might even retort—the wholly other is no longer wholly other because the impossible has become possible.¹³ In short, there can be no Immanuel, for "God with us" is an unthinkable proposition for deconstruction. Moreover, were Messiah ever to show up, there would be nothing left for which to hope.¹⁴ To insist that God *has come*—think here of the incarnational birth of Christ over two millennia ago, very much on my mind as I pen these words a week before Christmas—and to predicate one's belief on a Christ-centered eschatology are, for Derrida, knowledge-based actions that run

---

9. Tacey, "Jacques Derrida," 5.

10. Caputo, *Prayers and Tears of Jacques Derrida*, 7.

11. One here is reminded of Jesus's warning against false Christs: "At that time if anyone says to you, 'Look, here is the Messiah!' or, 'There he is!' do not believe it. For false messiahs and false prophets will appear and perform great signs and wonders to deceive, if possible, even the elect. See, I have told you ahead of time. So if anyone tells you, 'There he is, out in the wilderness,' do not go out; or, 'Here he is, in the inner rooms,' do not believe it" (Matt 24:23–26).

12. Peterson, *Five Smooth Stones for Pastoral Work*, 84.

13. Derrida, *On the Name*, 74.

14. Caputo, "Apostles of the Impossible," 186.

Conclusion

counter to true faith as he understood it. Inspired by Kierkegaard's efforts to demythologize the institutional beliefs and practices of European Christianity, Derrida nonetheless advocated the "de-Christification" of spirituality as an antidote to idolatry.[15] But lest he be thought of as antichristian, Derrida memorably insisted in another place, "What has not yet arrived at or happened to Christianity is Christianity. Christianity has not yet come to Christianity."[16] As we saw earlier, Derridean deconstruction, in paradoxically welcoming the messianic while resisting and refusing a robust Christology—perhaps even welcoming a "Christianity" of its own making, a Christianity without Christ—maintains this tension through its sustained commitment to aporia and undecidability. In a word, deconstruction is agnostic in its commitments.

Crucially, we also saw that deconstruction's embrace of undecidability is not something it has happily pursued but constitutes a heavy burden—his cross, as Derrida once put it[17]—that it, that he, cannot refuse to shoulder. Or perhaps it is a cross he *would not* lay down, given deconstruction's insistence, correctly so, that undecidability does not at all mean that no decisions can ever take place because faith is all about making decisions—hard difficult choices—amid conditions of undecidability. But rather than choosing Christ, Derridean deconstruction persists in its endless wait without waiting. Thus understood, aporia and undecidability are not gifts of grace for Derrida, but irrepressibly toilsome burdens.[18] Absent Christology in its reasoning, there can be no divine exchange as such for deconstruction since, by virtue of its embargo of all revelation, it remains tone deaf to Christ's invitation to the weary and burdened to find rest for their souls by taking on his easy yoke and light burden (Matt 11:28–30). Finally, in its wait for an impossible God who cannot be known nor named,[19] deconstruction seems to land in a place both surprising and not so surprising: the *self*. Recall that with the interiorization that occurs when the wholly other is prevented by deconstruction from ever speaking—when, as Richard Kearney has observed, God is deprived of the power to act and call and love because he

---

15. Derrida, *Specters of Marx*, 59.
16. Derrida, *Specters of Marx*, 28.
17. Kearney, "On the Gift," 73.
18. Hart, "Absolute Interruption," 202.

19. This is not quite the same as J. K. Rowling's Voldemort, "He Who Must Not Be Named," as deconstruction would reject the "You Know Who" that implies the Dark Lord was a known and knowable entity!

has been so distanced from his own creation as to be defunct[20]—Derrida seemed to end with the idolization and deification of his own self, where he and God, where self and other, are one and the same. For instance, in the "secret relationship" he has with himself and the God from which or whom nothing can be known or revealed, Derrida is left with this singular conclusion: "...once there is secrecy and secret witnessing within me, then what I call God exists, (there is) what I call God in me, (it happens that) *I call myself God*."[21] On the one hand, this outcome is surprising given deconstruction's relentless openness to and pursuit of otherness, indeed the wholly other no less. On the other hand, to where else might deconstruction's quest lead, given its absolute emasculation of the messianic by refusing God any agency? Fair or otherwise, such a conclusion does not imply that deconstruction intended to end with a self that is untouched and unchanged by otherness. As Caputo has insisted, deconstruction proceeds in the dark, not unlike how a blind person gingerly finds his way with a walking stick, "devoid of sight and savvy, of vision and verity . . . where it is necessary to believe, where the passion of faith . . . is all you have to go on."[22] For all the good it does—and there is a lot of that—deconstruction, tragically it seems, is but a blind man fueled by a passionate faith in nothing and trapped within his own darkness, when the world around him is filled with light (Isa 9:2).

The conversation closes, in the fourth chapter, by emphasizing the unequivocal claim of the Bible: God can be known! He desires to be known and acknowledged by his creation! And he invites women and men to be in close relationship and cooperative partnership with him! As the early Christian writer Tertullian once observed, "God neither could have been, nor ought to have been, unknown. Could not have been, because of His greatness; ought not to have been, because of His goodness . . ."[23] Against deconstruction's conception of a wholly other of whom or which nothing can or should be known, the God of the Bible readily reveals and avails of himself—progressively and selectively, to be sure, but he can be and has been known. Granted, there have been embargos of revelation; think, for instance, of the four hundred years of divine silence during the intertestamental period. But there is no denying the divine invitation for a time such

20. Kearney, "God Who May Be," 158.
21. Derrida, *Gift of Death*, 109, italics mine.
22. Caputo, *Prayers and Tears of Jacques Derrida*, xxvi.
23. Tertullian, *Writings of Tertullian*, 65.

CONCLUSION

as this: "Today, if only you would hear his voice . . ." (Ps 95:7b). Through his Word, God invites—indeed, he enjoins—us to come, call, ask, seek, and knock. Contrary to deconstruction's insistence on nothingness—"Nothing happens, nobody comes, nobody goes, it's awful!" as Beckett's protagonist frustratingly notes in *Waiting for Godot*—the biblical narrative portrays a world full of life and activity, with God busy at work fulfilling his promises made to his creation. Where the impossible God of deconstruction says and does nothing—indeed, the messianic in deconstruction is fully emasculated and deprived of agency—the biblical God of the impossible, Jesus of Nazareth no less, declares that there is nothing that is too hard or difficult for him to accomplish because all things are possible with him. And if all things are possible with Christ, then surely they include the possibility that humankind's propensity to objectify God and his revelation through metaphysics can in fact be mitigated by remaining within the immediacy and intimacy of responsive dialogue and relationship with God—"Remain in me, as I also remain in you" (John 15:4a)—and avoiding the temptation to distance ourselves from God. As Kevin Hart has correctly noted, the followers of Christ reside in a space of acknowledgment rather than of knowledge, where the conjunction of faith and reason never, despite our vainest efforts, resolves itself in favor of knowledge because God eludes all human and institutional attempts at metaphysical capture and domestication.[24] Or as Walter Brueggemann has put it, "It is enough to acknowledge, be awed, and delighted."[25] Secondly, in contrast to deconstruction's contention that God is always structurally *to come*—that a God who has already pitched his tent among us in the flesh is no God at all—another condition of possibility in Christ, per the logic of progressive revelation, could be that the returning Christ might be unrecognizable even to his most ardent and reverent worshipers who cry, "Maranatha!"[26] In other words, contra deconstruction, the Parousia spoken of in the New Testament may not consist in a complete givenness without surprises because Christian eschatology, when properly rooted in the Word of God and linked to a living and active faith, is the farthest thing from the sort of totalizing teleology that correctly worries the deconstructionists. It should worry us all.

---

24. Hart, "Absolute Interruption," 202.

25. Brueggemann, *Texts Under Negotiation*, 29.

26. If anything, the litmus test identified in Scripture is whether the Lord knows us and not only whether we know him (John 10:14).

Awaiting the Impossible

Despite its persistent yes to life, deconstruction stops short at saying yes to the crucified Christ, whom it seems to view as both a stumbling block and foolishness. That said, it has much that is extremely helpful, as we have seen, for reminding and warning the Christ-disciple of the dangers of predicating one's Christian faith less in the living Word of God than in the faux confidence of modernity that continues to guide many a Christian witness to postmodern audiences—a witness that seem to care neither for what the Bible says about the human condition nor the good tidings of great joy it offers. On the other hand, postmodern folks may just welcome Christ—when they see Christians set aside our false confidences and take seriously the cross-examined life that Jesus enjoins us to live daily, with unvarnished honesty and in sincere humility. For has God not shown us mortals that which is good? For what is it that the Lord requires of us, but to act justly, to love mercy, and to walk humbly with him (Mic 6:6–8)? In like vein, the posture of Derrida's eschatology is not one of chest-thumping confidence but rather of tear-streaked humility. In the conclusion to his *Memoirs of the Blind*, Derrida, averring that it is tears and not sight that are the essence of the eye, offered this thought: "Tears that see . . . Do you believe? I don't know, one has to believe."[27] In the light of the divine promise that the poor in spirit, the ones who mourn, and the pure in heart shall inherit the kingdom of heaven, be comforted, and even see God (i.e., the Beatitudes in Matt 5:3–12), is it not conceivable that Derrida and the deconstruction he introduced and vigorously practiced were on the right trek toward the holy—perhaps even toward Christ, even if, as we have seen, Derrida seemed to prefer a Christless Christianity? "Perhaps," as Derrida, the sly old fox that he was, might say.[28]

---

27. Derrida, *Memoirs of the Blind*, 129.
28. Derrida, *Politics of Friendship*, 29.

Bibliography

Alford, C. Fred. "Bauman and Levinas: Levinas Cannot Be Used." *Journal for Cultural Research* 18 (2014) 249–62.
Aristotle. *Metaphysics*. Translated by W. D. Ross with introduction by Edith Johnson. Overland Park, KS: Digireads, 2018.
Augustine. *Revisions (Retractationes) including an Appendix with the "Indiculus" of Possidius*. Edited by Roland J. Teske and translated by Boniface Ramsey. Hyde Park, NY: New City, 2010.
Barber, Daniel Colucciello. *Deleuze and the Naming of God: Postsecularism and the Future of Immanence*. Edinburgh: Edinburgh University Press, 2014.
Baring, Edward. *The Young Derrida and French Philosophy, 1945–1968*. Cambridge: Cambridge University Press, 2011.
Barth, Karl. *Epistle to the Romans*. Translated by Edwyn C. Hoskyns, sixth edition. Oxford: Oxford University Press, 1933.
Berman, Russell. "Kamala Harris Might Have to Stop the Steal." *The Atlantic*. October 6, 2021. https://www.theatlantic.com/politics/archive/2021/10/kamala-harris-trump-january-6/620310/.
Biemiller, Marc. "Augustine and Plato: Clarifying Misconceptions." *Aporia* 29, no. 2 (2019): 33–34.
Brooks, Arthur C. "Don't Shun Conservative Professors." *The New York Times*. September 15, 2017. https://www.nytimes.com/2017/09/15/opinion/conservative-professors.html.
Bonhoeffer, Dietrich. *Who Am I?* Minneapolis, MN: Augsburg, 2005.
Bonnke, Reinhard. *Evangelism by Fire: Keys for Effectively Reaching Others with the Gospel*. Lake Mary, FL: Charisma House, 2011.
Botha, Catherine F. "From Destruktion to Deconstruction: A Response to Moran." *South African Journal of Philosophy* 27 (2008) 52–68.
Bowler, Maurice G. "Rosenzweig on Judaism and Christianity—The Two Covenant Theory." *Judaism* 22 (1973) 475–481.
Brueggemann, Walter. *Theology of the Old Testament: Testimony, Dispute, Advocacy*. Minneapolis, MN: Fortress, 1977.
———. *Texts Under Negotiation: The Bible and Postmodern Imagination*. Minneapolis, MN: Fortress, 1973.
Buber, Martin. *Moses: The Revelation and the Covenant*. New York: Harper and Row, 1958.
Bultmann, Rudolf. *New Testament Mythology and Other Basic Writings*. Edited and translated by Schubert M. Ogden. Philadelphia, PA: Fortress, 1984.

Bibliography

Burley, Mikel. "Dislocating the Eschaton? Appraising Realized Eschatology." *Sophia* 56 (2017) 435–52.

Butler, Judith. *Bodies That Matter: On the Discursive Limits of Sex.* London: Routledge, 1993.

Campillo, Antonio. "Foucault and Derrida—The History of a Debate on History." *Angelaki: Journal of the Theoretical Humanities* 5 (2000) 113–35.

Caputo, John D. *Against Ethics: Contributions to a Poetics of Obligation with Constant Reference to Deconstruction.* Bloomington, IN: Indiana University Press, 1993.

———. "Apostles of the Impossible: On God and the Gift in Derrida and Marion." In *God, The Gift, and Postmodernism*, edited by John D. Caputo and Michael John Scanlon, 185–222. Bloomington, IN: Indiana University Press, 1999.

———. "A Community without Truth: Derrida and the Impossible Community." *Research in Phenomenology* 26 (1996) 25–37.

———. "Hyperbolic Justice: Deconstruction, Myth, and Politics." *Research in Phenomenology* 2 (1991) 3–20.

———. "Jacques Derrida (1930–2004)." *Journal for Cultural and Religious Theory* 6 (2004) 6–9.

———. "The Power of the Powerless: Dialogue with John D. Caputo." In *After the Death of God*, by John D. Caputo and Gianni Vattimo and edited by Jeffrey W. Robbins, 114–60. New York: Columbia University Press, 2007.

———. *The Prayers and Tears of Jacques Derrida: Religion without Religion.* Bloomington, IN: Indiana University Press, 1997.

———. "Spectral Hermeneutics: On the Weakness of God and the Theology of the Event." In *After the Death of God*, by John D. Caputo and Gianni Vattimo and edited by Jeffrey W. Robbins, 47–85. New York: Columbia University Press, 2007.

———. *The Weakness of God: A Theology of the Event.* Bloomington, IN: Indiana University Press, 2006.

———. "What Do I Love When I Love My God? Deconstruction and Radical Orthodoxy." In *Questioning God*, edited by John D. Caputo, Mark Dooley, and Michael J. Scanlon, 291–317. Bloomington, IN: Indiana University Press, 2001.

———. *What Would Jesus Deconstruct? The Good News of Postmodernism for the Church.* Grand Rapids, MI: Baker Academic, 2007.

Caputo, John D., and Michael John Scanlon. "Introduction: Apology for the Impossible: Religion and Postmodernism." In *God, The Gift, and Postmodernism*, edited by John D. Caputo and Michael John Scanlon, 1–19. Bloomington, IN: Indiana University Press, 1999.

Chan, Francis, with Danae Yankoski. *Crazy Love: Overwhelmed by a Relentless God.* Revised and update edition. Colorado Springs, CO: David C. Cook, 2013.

Chang, Curtis. *Engaging Unbelief: A Captivating Strategy from Augustine and Aquinas.* Downers Grove, IL: InterVarsity, 2000.

Chalier, Catherine. "Levinas and the Talmud." In *The Cambridge Companion to Levinas*, edited by Simon Critchley and Robert Bernasconi, 100–18. Cambridge: Cambridge University Press, 2002.

Cixous, Hélène. *Portrait of Jacques Derrida as a Young Jewish Saint.* Translated by Beverley Bie Brahic. New York: Columbia University Press, 2004.

Collins, Guy. "Thinking the Impossible: Derrida and the Devine." *Literature and Theology* 14, no. 3 (2000) 313–34.

Bibliography

Congdon, David W. "Bonhoeffer and Bultmann: Toward an Apocalyptic Rapprochement." *International Journal of Systematic Theology* 15 (2013) 172–95.

Connolly, William E. *Capitalism and Christianity, American Style*. Durham, NC: Duke University Press, 2008.

———. *William E. Connolly: Democracy, Pluralism and Political Theory*, eds. Samuel A Chambers, Terrell Carver. London: Routledge, 2008.

Critchley, Simon. "Introduction." In *The Cambridge Companion to Levinas*, edited by Simon Critchley and Robert Bernasconi, 1–32. Cambridge: Cambridge University Press, 2002.

Crockett, Clay. "Postmodernism and Its Secrets: Religion Without Religion." *CrossCurrents* 52 (2003) 499–515.

De Ville, Jacques. "Madness and the Law: The Derrida/Foucault Debate Revisited." *Law and Critique* 21 (2010) 17–37.

Deleuze, Gilles. *The Logic of Sense*. Edited by Constantin V. Boundas and translated by Mark Lester with Charles Stivale. New York: Columbia University Press, 1969.

Derrida, Jacques. *Adieu to Emmanuel Levinas*. Translated by Pascale-Anne Brault and Michael Naas. Stanford, CA: Stanford University Press, 1990.

———. *The Animal that Therefore I Am*. Edited by Marie-Louise Mallet and David Wills and translated by David Wills. New York: Fordham University Press, 2008.

———. "Circumfession." In *Jacques Derrida*, by Geoffrey Bennington and Jacques Derrida, 3–315. Chicago, IL: University of Chicago Press, 1993.

———. "Cogito and the History of Madness." In *Writing and Difference*, translated and with an introduction by Alan Bass, 31–63. Chicago, IL: University of Chicago Press, 1978.

———. *On Cosmopolitanism and Forgiveness (Thinking in Action)*. London: Routledge, 1998.

———. *Deconstruction in a Nutshell: A Conversation with Jacques Derrida*. Edited by John D. Caputo. New York: Fordham University Press, 1997.

———. *Derrida and Negative Theology*. Edited by Harold Coward and Toby Foshay. Albany, NY: SUNY Press, 1992.

———. "Différance." In *Margins of Philosophy*, translated by Alan Bass, 3–27. Chicago, IL: University of Chicago Press, 1982.

———. "Faith and Knowledge: The Two Sources of 'Religion' at the Limits of Mere Reason." In *Religion*, edited by Jacques Derrida and Gianni Vattimo and translated by Samuel Weber. Stanford, CA: Stanford University Press, 1998.

———. "Force of Law: The 'Mystical Foundation of Authority.'" In *Deconstruction and the Possibility of Justice*, edited by Drucilla Cornell, Michel Rosenfeld, and David Gray Carlson, 3–67. London: Routledge, 1992.

———. *The Gift of Death*. Edited by Mark C. Taylor and translated by David Wills. Chicago, IL: Chicago University Press, 1995.

———. *Given Time: I. Counterfeit Money*. Translated by P. Kamuf. Chicago, IL: University of Chicago Press, 2017.

———. "Hostipitality." In *Acts of Religion*, edited by Gil Anidjar, 356–420. London: Routledge, 2002.

———. *Learning to Live Finally: The Last Interview*. Translated by Pascale-Anne Brault and Michael Naas. Hoboken, NJ: Melville House, 2007.

———. *Memoires: For Paul de Man*. Revised edition. New York: Columbia University Press, 1989.

Bibliography

———. *Memoirs of the Blind: The Self-Portrait and Other Ruins*. Translated by Pascale-Anne Brault and Michael Naas. Chicago, IL: University of Chicago Press, 1993.

———. "Of an Apocalyptic Tone Recently Adopted in Philosophy." In *Semeia 23: Derrida and Biblical Studies*, edited by Robert Detweiler. Chico, CA: Society of Biblical Literature, 1982.

———. *Of Grammatology*. Edited and translated by Gayatri Chakravorty Spivak. Baltimore, MD: Johns Hopkins University Press, 1976.

———. *On the Name*. Edited by Thomas Dutoit and translated by David Wood, John P. Leavey, Jr., and Ian McLeod. Stanford, CA: Stanford University Press, 1995.

———. "La parole—Donner, nommer, appeler." In *Paul Ricoeur*, edited by Myriam Revault d'Allonnes and Francois Azouvi. Paris: Editions de L'Herne, 2004.

———. *Points… Interviews, 1974–1994*. Edited by Elisabeth Weber and translated by Peggy Kamuf and others. Stanford, CA: Stanford University Press, 1995.

———. *The Politics of Friendship*. Translated by George Collins. New York: Verso, 2005.

———. *Positions*. Translated and annotated by Alan Bass. Chicago, IL: University of Chicago Press, 1981.

———. *The Post Card: From Socrates to Freud and Beyond*. Translated by Alan Bass. Chicago, IL: University of Chicago Press, 1987.

———. *The Problem of Genesis in Husserl's Philosophy*. Translated by Marian Hobson. Chicago, IL: University of Chicago Press, 1990.

———. *Questioning Ethics: Contemporary Debates in Continental Philosophy*. Edited by Mark Dooley and Richard Kearney. London: Routledge, 1999.

———. *Rogues: Two Essays in Reason*. Translated by Pascale-Ann Brault and Michael Naas. Stanford, CA: Stanford University Press, 2005.

———. *Specters of Marx: The State of the Debt, the Work of Mourning and the New International*. Translated by Peggy Kamuf. London: Routledge, 1993.

———. "Some Statements and Truisms about Neologisms, Newisms, Postisms, Parasitisms, and other Small Seismisms." In *The States of Theory*, edited by David Carroll, 63–94. New York: Columbia University Press, 1989.

———. "Violence and Metaphysics: An Essay on the Thought of Emmanuel Levinas." In *Writing and Difference*, translated and with an introduction by Alan Bass, 79–153. Chicago, IL: University of Chicago Press, 1978.

Derrida, Jacques, and Richard Beardsworth. "Nietzsche and the Machine." *Journal of Nietzsche Studies* 7 (1994) 7–66.

Derrida, Jacques, and John D. Caputo. "Justice, If Such a Thing Exists." In *Deconstruction in a Nutshell: A Conversation with Jacques Derrida*, edited by John D. Caputo, 125–55. New York: Fordham University Press, 1997.

Dilday, K. A. "Jacques Derrida: Life Beyond the Margins." *Open Democracy*. October 20, 2004. https://www.opendemocracy.net/en/2169/.

Dix, G. H. "The Messiah Ben Joseph." *The Journal of Theological Studies* 27 (1926): 130–43.

Dore, Isaak I. "Deconstructing and Reconstructing Hobbes." *Louisiana Law Review* 72 (2012) 815–71.

Dostoevsky, Fyodor. *Notes from Underground*. Translated by Richard Pevear and Larissa Volokhonsky. New York: Vintage, 1994.

Evans, Fred. "Derrida and the Autoimmunity of Democracy." *The Journal of Speculative Philosophy* 30 (2016) 303–15.

Findlay, Edward F. *Caring for the Soul in a Postmodern Age: Politics and Phenomenology in the Thought of Jan Patočka*. Albany, NY: SUNY Press, 2012.

Bibliography

Foucault, Michel. *History of Madness.* Edited by Jean Khalfa. London: Routledge, 2006.

Frank, Joseph. *Dostoevsky: The Mantle of the Prophet, 1871–1881, Volume 5.* Princeton, NJ: Princeton University Press, 2002.

Fritsch, Matthias. "Derrida's Democracy To Come." *Constellations: An International Journal of Critical and Democratic Theory* 9 (2002) 574–97.

Fukuyama, Francis. *The End of History and the Last Man.* New York: Free, 1992.

Galli, Mark. "The Heart of the Evangelical Crisis." *Christianity Today.* May 15, 2019. https://www.christianitytoday.com/ct/2019/may-web-only/elusive-presence-1-heart-of-evangelical-crisis.html.

Ganssle, Gregory E. *Our Deepest Desires: How the Christian Story Fulfills Human Aspirations.* Downers Grove, IL: InterVarsity, 2017.

Garrard, Graeme. "Nietzsche for and against the Enlightenment." *The Review of Politics* 70 (2008) 595–608.

Gasché, Rodolphe. "European Memories: Jan Patočka and Jacques Derrida on Responsibility." *Critical Inquiry* 33 (2007) 291–311.

Goldman, Peter. "Christian Mystery and Responsibility Gnosticism in Derrida's *The Gift of Death.*" *Anthropoetics: The Journal of Generative Anthropology* 4 (1999) 1–11.

Gray, John. *Liberalism.* Second edition. Minneapolis, MN: University of Minnesota Press, 1995.

Guarino, Thomas. *Vattimo and Theology.* New York: Continuum, 2009.

Hanson, Jeffrey. "A Tale of Two Doublets: Derrida and Kierkegaard." *Journal of Cultural and Religious Theory* 10 (2010) 54–63.

Hanson, Jeffrey. "Returning (to) The Gift of Death: Violence and History in Derrida and Levinas." *International Journal for Philosophy of Religion* 67 (2010) 1–15.

Hart, Kevin. "Absolute Interruption." In *Questioning God*, edited by John D. Caputo, Mark Dooley, and Michael J. Scanlon, 186–208. Bloomington, IN: Indiana University Press, 2001.

Hill, Leslie. *Maurice Blanchot and Fragmentary Writing: A Change of Epoch.* New York: Continuum, 2012.

Hobbes. *The Leviathan,* 1660. https://www.ttu.ee/public/m/mart-murdvee/EconPsy/6/Hobbes_Thomas_1660_The_Leviathan.pdf.

Hoffman, John P., Bruce R. Lott, and Catherine Jeppsen. "Religious Giving and the Boundedness of Rationality." *Sociology of Religion* 71 (2010) 323–48.

Horton, Michael S. *Covenant and Eschatology: The Divine Drama.* Louisville, KY: Westminster John Knox, 2002.

Hudson, W. Donald. "The Concept of Divine Transcendence." *Religious Studies* 15 (1979) 197–210.

Hunter, Ian. *Malcolm Muggeridge: A Life.* Nashville, TN: Thomas Nelson, 1980.

Huntington, Samuel P. "The Clash of Civilizations?" *Foreign Affairs* 72 (1993) 22–49.

Kahn, Paul W. *Putting Liberalism in Its Place.* Princeton, NJ: Princeton University Press, 2004.

Kearney, Richard. "Desire of God." In *God, The Gift, and Postmodernism*, edited by John D. Caputo and Michael John Scanlon, 112–45. Bloomington, IN: Indiana University Press, 1999.

———. "Ethics and the Postmodern Imagination." *Thought: Fordham University Quarterly* 62 (1987) 39–58.

Bibliography

———. "On Forgiveness: A Roundtable Discussion with Jacques Derrida, Moderated by Richard Kearney." In *Questioning God*, edited by John D. Caputo, Mark Dooley, and Michael J. Scanlon, 52–72. Bloomington, IN: Indiana University Press, 2001.

———. "On the Gift: A Discussion with Jacques Derrida and Jean-Luc Marion." In *God, The Gift, and Postmodernism*, edited by John D. Caputo and Michael John Scanlon, 57–78. Bloomington, IN: Indiana University Press, 1999.

———. "The God Who May Be." In *Questioning God*, edited by John D. Caputo, Mark Dooley, and Michael J. Scanlon, 153–85. Bloomington, IN: Indiana University Press, 2001.

Kenney, John Peter. "'None Come Closer to Us than These': Augustine and the Platonists." *Religions* 7.9 (2016). https://doi.org/10.3390/rel7090114.

Kierkegaard, Søren. *Fear and Trembling*. Morrisville, NC: Lulu, 2018.

———. *Søren Kierkegaard's Journals and Papers, Volume 1*. Translated by Hoard V. Hong, Edna Hong, and Gregor Melantschuk. Bloomington, IN: Indiana University Press, 1967–78.

Kim, Chin-Tai. "Transcendence and Immanence." *Journal of the American Academy of Religion* 55 (1987) 537–49.

Kostecki-Shaw, Jenny Sue. *Same, Same But Different*. New York: Macmillan, 2011.

Kubicki, Judith M. *The Presence of Christ in the Gathered Assembly*. London and New York: Bloomsbury, 2006.

Kurlander, Eric. *Living with Hitler: Liberal Democrats in the Third Reich*. New Haven, CT: Yale University Press, 2009.

Labarthe, Philippe Lacoue. *Typography: Mimesis, Philosophy, Politics*. Cambridge, MA: Harvard University Press, 1998.

LaCocque, Andre. "The Revelation of Revelations." In *Thinking Biblically: Exegetical and Hermeneutical Studies*, by Andre LaCocque and Paul Ricoeur and translated by David Pellauer, 307–30. Chicago, IL: University of Chicago Press, 1998.

Leitch, Vincent B. "Review: Excess: Second Lives of Jacques Derrida." *SubStance* 41 (2012) 146–56.

Lewis, C. S. *The Weight of Glory, and Other Addresses*. Grand Rapids, MI: Zondervan, 2001.

Levinas, Emmanuel. *Ethique et infini*. Paris: Le livre de poche, 2000.

———. *Of God Who Comes to Mind*. Translated by Bettina Bergo. Stanford, CA: Stanford University Press, 1998.

———. *Otherwise Than Being or Beyond Essence*. Translated by Alphonso Lingis. Boston, MA: Kluwer Academic, 1991.

———. *Totality and Infinity: An Essay on Exteriority*. Translated by Alphonso Lingis. Pittsburgh, PA: Duquesne University Press, 1969.

Levinas, Emmanuel, and Sean Hand. "Reflections on the Philosophy of Hitlerism." *Critical Inquiry* 17 (1990) 62–71.

Levinas, Emmanuel, and Richard Kearney. "Dialogue with Emmanuel Levinas." In *Face to Face with Levinas*, edited by Richard A. Cohen, 13–34. Albany, NY: SUNY Press, 1986.

Lijster, Thijs. "'All Reification Is a Forgetting': Benjamin, Adorno, and the Dialectic of Reification." In *The Spell of Capital: Reification and Spectacle*, edited by Samir Gandesha and Johan F. Hart, 55–66. Amsterdam: Amsterdam University Press, 2017.

Looper, Terry. *Sacred Pace: Four Steps to Hearing God and Aligning Yourself with His Will*. Nashville, TN: Thomas Nelson, 2019.

Bibliography

Luther, Martin. *A Commentary on St. Paul's Epistle to the Galatians by Martin Luther.* Translated by Theodore Graebner. Morrisville, NC: Lulu, 2007.

———. *Luther's Works, Volume 10: Lectures on the Psalms I (I-75).* Edited by Hilton C. Oswald and translated by Herbert J. A. Bouman. St. Louis, MO: Concordia, 1974.

Lyotard, Jean-François. *The Postmodern Condition: A Report on Knowledge.* Translated by Geoff Bennington and Brian Massumi with a foreword by Fredric Jameson. Minneapolis, MN: University of Minnesota Press, 1984.

Maimonides, Moses. *The Guide for the Perplexed.* Translated by M. Friedlander. New York: Dover, 1956.

Marion, Jean-Luc. *God Without Being.* Translated by Thomas A. Carlson. Chicago, IL: University of Chicago Press, 1991.

———. "In His Name: How to Avoid Speaking of 'Negative Theology.'" In *God, The Gift, and Postmodernism,* edited by John D. Caputo and Michael John Scanlon, 20–53. Bloomington, IN: Indiana University Press, 1999.

Marsden, George M. *The Soul of the American University: From the Protestant Establishment to Established Nonbelief.* New York: Oxford University Press, 1994.

Martel, James. "Waiting for Justice: Benjamin and Derrida on Sovereignty and Immanence." *Republics of Letters: A Journal for the Study of Knowledge, Politics, and the Arts* 2 (2011) 158–72.

Mason, Mike. *The Gospel According to Job: An Honest Look at Pain and Doubt from the Life of One Who Lost Everything.* Wheaton, IL: Crossway, 1994.

Mauss, Marcel. *The Gift: The Form and Reason for Exchange in Archaic Societies.* Translated by W. D. Halls. London: Routledge, 1990.

McKelway, Alexander J. *The Systematic Theology of Paul Tillich: A Review and Analysis.* Louisville, KY: John Knox, 1965.

Metaxas, Eric. *Martin Luther: The Man Who Rediscovered God and Changed the World.* New York: Penguin Books, 2017.

Metz, Johann Baptist. *Faith in History and Society: Toward a Practical Fundamental Theology.* Translated by J. Matthew Ashley. New York: Herder and Herder, 2007.

Monte, Jonas. "Sum, Ergo Cogito: Nietzsche Re-orders Descartes." *Aporia* 25 (2015) 13–22.

Morgan, Michael L. *The Cambridge Introduction to Emmanuel Levinas.* Cambridge: Cambridge University Press, 2011.

Morin, Marie-Eve. "The Self, The Other, and the Many: Derrida on Testimony." *Mosaic: An Interdisciplinary Critical Journal* 40 (2007) 165–78.

Mouffe, Chantel (Ed.) *The Challenge of Carl Schmitt.* London: Verso, 1999.

Moreland, J. P. *Scientism and Secularism: Learning to Respond to a Dangerous Ideology.* Wheaton, IL: Crossway, 2018.

Muggeridge, Malcolm. *Something Beautiful for God: The Classic Account of Mother Teresa's Journey into Compassion.* San Francisco, CA: Harper and Row, 2003.

Murray, Douglas. *Neoconservatism: Why We Need It.* New York: Encounter, 2005.

Nancy, Jean-Luc. *Dis-Enclosure: The Deconstruction of Christianity.* Translated by Bettina Bergo, Gabriel Malenfant, and Michael B. Smith. New York: Fordham University Press, 2008.

Narveson, Jan. *The Libertarian Idea.* Philadelphia, PA: Temple University Press, 1988.

Neie, Herbert. *The Doctrine of the Atonement in the Theology of Wolfhart Pannenberg.* New York: Walter De Gruyter, 1979.

Bibliography

Newman, Randy. *Bringing the Gospel Home: Witnessing to Family Members, Close Friends, and Others Who Know You Well.* Wheaton, IL: Crossway, 2011.

Nietzsche, Friedrich. *Beyond Good and Evil.* New York: Cosimo, 2006.

———. *Ecce Homo.* Translated by Anthony Ludovici. London: T. N. Foulis, 1911.

———. *On the Genealogy of Morality.* Edited by Keith Ansell-Pearson and translated by Carol Diethe. Cambridge: Cambridge University Press, 2006.

———. *The Will to Power.* Edited and translated by R. Kevin Hill and Michael A. Scarpitti. London: Penguin, 2017.

Norris, Christopher. *Deconstruction: Theory and Practice.* Third edition. London: Routledge, 2004.

Nussbaum, Martha C. "Objectification." *Philosophy & Public Affairs* 24 (1995) 249–91.

Oksala, Johanna. *Foucault on Freedom.* Cambridge: Cambridge University Press, 2005.

O'Leary, Joseph S. *Questioning Back: The Overcoming of Metaphysics in Christian Tradition.* Minneapolis, MN: Winston, 1985.

Otto, Rudolf. *The Idea of the Holy.* Translated by John W. Harvey. Oxford: Oxford University Press, 1923.

Pagels, Elaine. *The Gnostic Gospels.* New York: Vintage, 1989.

Pannenberg, Wolfhart. *Anthropology in Theological Perspective.* Philadelphia, PA: Westminster, 1985.

Patai, Raphael. *The Messiah Texts.* Detroit, MI: Wayne State University Press, 1979.

Patočka, Jan. *Heretical Essays in the Philosophy of History.* Edited by James Dodd and translated by Erazim Kohak. Chicago, IL: University of Chicago Press, 1996.

Peeters, Benoit. *Derrida: A Biography.* Translated by Andrew Brown. Cambridge: Polity, 2013.

Pennington, Jonathan T. *The Sermon on the Mount and Human Flourishing: A Theological Commentary.* Grand Rapids, MI: Baker Academic, 2017.

Peterson, Eugene. *Five Smooth Stones for Pastoral Work.* Grand Rapids, MI: Wm. B. Eerdmans, 1980.

Pfortmüller, Fabian. "Why Communities Based on Reciprocity are Selling Themselves Short." *Medium.* April 30, 2018. https://medium.com/@pforti/the-danger-of-reciprocity-based-communities-d328446c7057.

Piper, John. "What's the Significance of Simon Carrying Jesus's Cross?" *Desiring God.* April 19, 2019. https://www.desiringgod.org/interviews/whats-the-significance-of-simon-carrying-jesuss-cross

Raffoul, Francois. "Heidegger and Derrida." In *The Bloomsbury Companion to Heidegger*, edited by Francois Raffoul and Eric S. Nelson, 401–08. London: A&C Black, 2013.

Rahner, Karl. "The Hermeneutics of Eschatological Assertions." *Theological Investigations* 4 (1954) 326–46.

Raschke, Carl A. *The Next Reformation: Why Evangelicals Must Embrace Postmodernity.* Grand Rapids, MI: Baker Academic, 2004.

Raschke, Carl, and Hale, David. "Not Your Grandmother's Theory of Religion: An Interview with Carl Raschke." *Journal of Cultural and Religious Theory* 14 (2014) 1–7.

Rawls, John. "Kantian Constructivism in Moral Theory." *Journal of Philosophy* 77 (1980) 515–72.

Rayment-Pickard, Hugh. *Impossible God: Derrida's Theology.* London: Routledge, 2003.

Robbins, Jeffrey W. "Introduction: After the Death of God." In *After the Death of God*, by John D. Caputo and Gianni Vattimo and edited by Jeffrey W. Robbins, 1–24. New York: Columbia University Press, 2007.

BIBLIOGRAPHY

Roberts, Tyler T. "Confessing Philosophy/Writing Grace: Derrida, Augustine, and the Practice of Deconstruction." *Soundings* 79 (1996) 3–4.

Royle, Nicholas. "Jacques Derrida, Also, Enters into Heaven." *Angelaki: Journal of the Theoretical Humanities* 3 (1998) 113–16.

Saghafi, Kas. "'An Almost Unheard-of Analogy': Derrida Reading Levinas." *Bulletin de Ja Société Américaine de Philosophie de Langue Française* 15 (2005) 41–71.

Said, Edward W. *Orientalism*. New York: Pantheon, 1979.

Scanlon, Michael. "A Deconstruction of Religion: On Derrida and Rahner." In *God, The Gift, and Postmodernism*, edited by John D. Caputo and Michael John Scanlon, 223–28. Bloomington, IN: Indiana University Press, 1999.

Scanlon, Thomas M. *What We Owe to Each Other*. Cambridge, MA: Harvard University Press, 1998.

Schopenhauer, Arthur. *The World as Will and Representation, Vol. 1*. Translated by E. F. J. Payne. Mineola, NY: Dover, 1996.

Schwartz, Regina Mara. "Questioning Narratives of God: The Immeasurable in Measures." In *Questioning God*, edited by John D. Caputo, Mark Dooley, and Michael J. Scanlon, 209–34. Bloomington, IN: Indiana University Press, 2001.

Schwarzschild, Steven S. *Franz Rosenzweig, 1886–1929: Guide to Reversioners*. London: Education Committee of the Hillel Foundation, 1960.

Seidel, Andrew L. "A Love Letter to #Exvangelicals and Those Deconstructing Their Toxic Faith." *Religious Dispatches*. September 20, 2021. https://religiondispatches.org/a-love-letter-to-exvangelicals-and-those-deconstructing-their-toxic-faith/

Shepherd, Andrew. *The Gift of the Other: Levinas, Derrida, and a Theology of Hospitality*. Eugene, OR: Pickwick, 2014.

Sigal, Phillip. "Aspects of Dual Covenant Theology: Salvation." *Horizons in Biblical Theology* 4 (1982) 1–48.

Smith, Dinitia. "Philosopher Gamely In Defense Of His Ideas." *The New York Times*. May 30, 1998. https://www.nytimes.com/1998/05/30/arts/philosopher-gamely-in-defense-of-his-ideas.html

Sokoloff, William W. "Between Justice and Legality: Derrida on Decision." *Political Research Quarterly* 58 (2005) 341–52.

Spencer, Jacob. "A Defense of the Metaphysics of Divine Simplicity as Explained by Thomas Aquinas." *Aporia* 30 (2000) 1–13.

Spivak, Gayatri Chakravorty. "Bonding in Difference: Interview with Alfred Arteaga (1993–94)." In *The Spivak Reader: Selected Works of Gayatri Chakravorty Spivak*, edited by Donna Landry and Gerald MacLean, 15–28. London: Routledge, 1996.

———. "Translator's Preface." In *Of Grammatology*. Corrected edition. By Jacques Derrida and translated by Gayatri Chakravorty Spivak, ix–lxxxvii. Baltimore, MD: Johns Hopkins Press, 1997.

Spong, John Shelby. *Resurrection: Myth or Reality? A Bishop's Search for the Origins of Christianity*. Revised edition. San Francisco, CA: HarperOne, 1995.

Sproul, R. C. *The Holiness of God*. Wheaton, IL: Tyndale House, 1985.

Stenner, Karen. "Three Kinds of 'Conservatism.'" *Psychological Inquiry* 20 (2009) 142–59.

Stephens, Mitchell. "Jacques Derrida." *The New York Times Magazine*. January 23, 1994. https://www.nytimes.com/1994/01/23/magazine/jacques-derrida.html

Stern, Thomas. *Nietzsche's Ethics*. Cambridge: Cambridge University Press, 2020.

Sturm, F. P. "Charles Baudelaire." In *Baudelaire: His Prose and Poetry*, edited by T. R. Smith, 11–36. New York: Boni and Liveright, 1919.

Bibliography

Swanson, David. *Rediscipling the White Church: From Cheap Diversity to True Solidarity.* Downers Grove, IL: InterVarsity, 2020.

Tacey, David. "Jacques Derrida: The Enchanted Atheist." *Thesis Eleven* 110, no. 1 (2012): 3–16.

Taylor, Mark C. "What Derrida Really Meant." *The New York Times.* October 14, 2004. https://www.nytimes.com/2004/10/14/opinion/what-derrida-really-meant.html.

Taylor, Victor E. "Altizer's Derrida: Apocalyptic Spectralities." *Journal for Cultural and Religious Theory* 19 (2019–20) 45–51.

———. "Divisible Derridas." *Journal of Cultural and Religious Theory* 6 (2004) 1–5.

———. "Jesus' Spectral Intervention: Derrida, Christianity, and 'Hauntology.'" *Journal of Cultural and Religious Theory* 17 (2017) 158–89.

Tertullian. *The Writings of Tertullian—Volume II.* Woodstock, ON: Devoted, 2017.

Teurlings, Monica. *Destination Self: Navigated for You with Love from My Spirit Guides.* Carlsbad, CA: Balboa, 2018.

Tillich, Paul. *Systematic Theology, Volume 1.* Chicago, IL: University of Chicago Press, 2012.

Vallie, Robert M. "Augustine Confessions and the Impossibility of Confessing God." *Auslegung: A Journal of Philosophy* 25 (2002) 37–62.

Vattimo, Gianni. "Toward a Nonreligious Christianity." In *After the Death of God*, by John D. Caputo and Gianni Vattimo and edited by Jeffrey W. Robbins, 27–46. New York: Columbia University Press, 2006.

Volf, Miroslav, and Matthew Croasmun. *For the Life of the World: Theology That Makes a Difference.* Grand Rapids, MI: Brazos, 2019.

Von Balthasar, Hans Urs. *Theo-Drama: Theological Dramatic Theory.* Translated by Graham Harrison. San Francisco, CA: Ignatius, 1988.

Waldenfels, Bernhard. "Levinas and the Face of the Other." In *The Cambridge Companion to Levinas*, edited by Simon Critchley and Robert Bernasconi, 63–81. Cambridge: Cambridge University Press, 2002.

Ward, Graham. *Barth, Derrida and the Language of Theology.* Cambridge: Cambridge University Press, 1995.

———. "Questioning God." In *Questioning God*, edited by John D. Caputo, Mark Dooley, and Michael J. Scanlon, 274–90. Bloomington, IN: Indiana University Press, 2001.

Ware, Owen. "Universality and Historicity: On the Sources of Religion." *Research in Phenomenology* 36 (2006) 238–54.

Warren, Tish Harrison. "The Church Needs Reformation, Not Deconstruction." *Christianity Today.* October 19, 2021. https://www.christianitytoday.com/ct/2021/november/exvangelical-warren-guide-to-deconstruction-church.html

Westphal, Merold. "Of God who comes to mind, by Emmanuel Levinas." *Modern Theology* 15 (1990) 522–24.

———. "Overcoming Onto-theology." In *God, The Gift, and Postmodernism*, edited by John D. Caputo and Michael John Scanlon, 146–69. Bloomington, IN: Indiana University Press, 1999.

———. *Suspicion and Faith: The Religious Uses of Modern Atheism.* Grand Rapids, MI: William B. Eerdmans, 1993.

Willaschek, Marcus. "Right and Coercion: Can Kant's Conception of Right Be Derived from His Moral Theory?" *International Journal of Philosophical Studies* 17 (2009) 49–70.

Williams, R. J. "Metaphysics and Metalepsis in *Thus Spoke Zarathustra*." *International Studies in Philosophy* 16 (1984) 27–36.
Woodberry, J. Dudley, Russell G. Shubin, and G. Marks. "Why Muslims Follow Jesus." *Christianity Today*. October 24, 2007. https://www.christianitytoday.com/ct/2007/october/42.80.html
Wright, Terry R. "Through a *Glas* Darkly: Derrida, Literature, and the Specter of Christianity." *Christianity and Literature* 44 (1994) 73–92.
Wyschogrod, Edith. "Eating the Text, Defiling the Hands: Specters in Arnold Schoenberg's Opera *Moses and Aron*." In *God, The Gift, and Postmodernism*, edited by John D. Caputo and Michael John Scanlon, 245–59. Bloomington, IN: Indiana University Press, 1999.
Yancey, Philip. *The Jesus I Never Knew*. Grand Rapids, MI: Zondervan, 2002.
Young, Robert. *Young's Analytical Concordance to the Bible*. Peabody, MA: Hendrickson, 2018.
Žižek, Slavoj. *The Fragile Absolute: Or, Why Is the Christian Legacy Worth Fighting For?* Second edition. London: Verso, 2009.

www.ingramcontent.com/pod-product-compliance
Lightning Source LLC
Chambersburg PA
CBHW072149160426
43197CB00012B/2306